A-Z EAST

CONTE

REFERENCE

A Road	A259
B Road	B2191
Dual Carriageway	
One-way Street Traffic flow on A roads is also indicated by a heavy line on the driver's left.	
Restricted Access	
Pedestrianized Road	
House Numbers A & B Roads only	10 124
Track & Footpath	
Residential Walkway	
Cycleway	
Railway	Level Crossing Station
Built-up Area	IVY LA.
Local Authority Boundary	
Posttown Boundary	
Postcode Boundary Within Posttown	
Map Continuation	16 Large Scale Town Centre 2

Car Park Selected	P
Church or Chapel	†
Fire Station	■
Hospital	H
Information Centre	i
National Grid Reference	565
Police Station	▲
Post Office	★
Toilet:	
without facilities for the disabled	
with facilities for the disabled	
for exclusive use by the disabled	
Viewpoint	
Educational Establishment	
Hospital, Hospice or Health Centre	
Industrial Building	
Leisure or Recreational Facility	
Place of Interest	
Public Building	
Shopping Centre or Market	
Other Selected Buildings	

SCALE

Map Pages 4-23 1:15,840

0 ¼ ½ Mile

0 250 500 750 Metres

4 inches (10.16cm) to 1 mile 6.31cm to 1km

Map Pages 2-3 1:7,920

0 ⅛ ¼ Mile

0 100 200 300 400 Metres

8 inches (20.32cm) to 1 mile 12.63cm to 1km

Copyright of Geographers' A-Z Map Company Ltd.

Head Office:
Fairfield Road, Borough Green, Sevenoaks, Kent TN15 8PP
Telephone: 01732 781000
www.a-zmaps.co.uk

Edition 3 2002 Edition 3A 2004 (part revision)

2
A
B
C
D
19
Old Town
HIGH ST. THE
A259
A2270
UPPERTON
GOFFS
Towner Art Gallery & Eastbourne Local History Museum
Manor Gardens
Playground
Bowling Grns.
GILDREDGE PARK
Tennis Courts
Eastbourne
The Saffrons (Cricket & Football Ground)
Library
Law Courts
Town Hall
Upperton Gdns.
Hartfield Square
A2040
ROYAL EASTBOURNE GOLF COURSE
Sports Ground
Club House
Temple Grove
Compton Place
COMPTON PARK
BN20
Trevin Towers
University of Brighton (Welkin Site)
University of Brighton (Hillbrow Site)
Bernersmede
Meads
Grange Gardens
Eastbourne Coll.
Pennell House
Playing Field
Eastbourne College
Gonville House (Eastbourne College)
CARLISLE ROAD
MEADS ROAD
SILVERDALE ROAD
BLACKWATER
GRANGE ROAD
JEVINGTON
OLD WISH
SAFFRONS ROAD
PARADISE DRIVE
COMPTON DRIVE
COMPTON PLACE ROAD
ARLINGTON ROAD
SOUTHFIELDS ROAD
TERMINUS ROAD
STATION RBT.
ENTERPRISE SHOPPING CENTRE
23
1
2
3
4
5
6
98
099
560

E
F
G
H
3
20
62
Mosque
Depot
Bourne Primary School
ITA Centre
YMCA
CAVENDISH AV.
BOURNE MEWS
BERWICK COURT
CROFT COURT
HURST COURT
THORNTON CT.
DORSET CT.
RAINEY COURT
GRAFTON CT.
CATOR HOUSE
BUSBY CT.
RIVERBOURNE HOUSE
WILLOWFIELD SQ.
WINDSOR CT.
LANCASTER CT.
PALGRAVE HO.
PHOENIX CT.
THE RESIDENCE
LINOSA CT.
BOURNESIDE COURT
RUSH COURT
SOLLY CT.
SYDNEY ROAD
MELBOURNE
NEW RD.
BELMORE RD.
BAYHAM RD.
HAMPDEN TER.
LATIMER RD.
ST. AUBYN'S
BURFIELD RD.
MARINE RD.
LEAF HALL RD.
METROPOLE CT.
MARINE PARADE
ROYAL PARADE
PROMENADE
BN22
BN21
SEASIDE
SEASIDE ROAD
A259
B2103
B2106
ASHFORD ROAD
SUSAN'S ROAD
ASHFORD SQUARE
LEAF ROAD
SUSAN'S RD.
LONGSTONE
WELLESLEY RD.
HARRIS CT.
TIDESWELL
TIDESWELL RD.
CAXTONS MS.
LANGNEY ROAD
PEVENSEY ROAD
NORTH ST.
JUNCTION ROAD
KILBURN TER.
EASTBOURNE
ARNDALE CENTRE
Synagogue
Curzon Cin.
Club
THE GRANGE
Bus Depot
BEVERLEY HO.
CEYLON PLACE
RENASCENT HO.
Royal Hippodrome Theatre
COLONNADE RD.
COLONNADE GDNS.
QUEEN'S GDS.
LION LA.
HAUGHTON HO.
CAVENDISH PL.
SUTTON RD.
TERMINUS ROAD
Sussex Gdns.
CORNFIELD ROAD
HYDE GARDENS
CONNAUGHT RD.
CHATSWORTH WALK
BOLTON ROAD
LISMORE ROAD
ALCISTON MS.
WINDERMERE COURT
HARFORD BATTERSBY HO.
LA RONDE CT.
TRINITY TREES
TERMINUS RD.
VICTORIA MANS.
ELMS AVENUE
AVENUE MANS.
GLADSTONE CT.
BURLINGTON RD.
ANDWELL CT.
WESTDOWN HOUSE
GANNET HO.
CLIVE CT.
GREENCROFT
SOVEREIGN HO.
ST. BRELADES
TRINITY PLACE
HARTINGTON PLACE
MEMORIAL RBT.
CLIFTON CT.
MAYFAIR HO.
VALENTINE CT.
SHERWOOD CT.
ESPERANCE HOSP.
SUSSEX HO.
HARTINGTON MANS.
BELTRY CT.
CHATSWORTH HO.
TAVISTOCK
DEVONSHIRE PLACE
PEARL CT.
BURLINGTON CT.
MERLYNN
ASHBOURNE CT.
PARK LODGE
BURLINGTON MANS.
GARDEN CT.
VICTORIA CT.
STREET
HARDWICK
WISH ROAD
CORNFIELD LANE
CORNFIELD TER.
Museum
PAULING HO.
BARCHESTER PL.
THORN LODGE
VERNON LODGE
SPENCER HOUSE
PARK LODGE
THE LODGE
CRANBORNE CT.
CLIFFORD HO.
PARK HO.
PARK GATES
WEST HOUSE
CHISWICK PL.
HOWARD SQUARE
HOWARD HOUSE
International Lawn Tennis Centre
Devonshire Park
Devonshire Park Fitness Cen.
Devonshire Park Theatre
Winter Garden
Congress Theatre
Heritage Cen.
MOWBRAY CT.
THE MANSIONS
LASCELLES MANS.
LASCELLES TER.
DEVONSHIRE MANS.
CARLISLE RD.
GRAND PARADE
MARINE PARADE
PARADE
LOWER PARADE
MIDDLE PARADE
The Carpet Gds.
Allchorn Pleasure Boats
Pier
Landing Stages
Bandstand
EASTBOURNE
099
ENGLISH CHANNEL
Lifeboat Mus.
BERKELEY COURT
GRAND COURT
WILMINGTON GDNS.
WILMINGTON SQUARE
CHURCHILL CT.
HAMPDEN CT.
LANSDOWNE CT.
LAMONT CT.
DARRICK CT.
LANCASTER HO.
KENTON CT.
JEVINGTON GDNS.
Martello Tower no.73
The Wish Tower
Puppet Museum
Western Lawns
KING EDWARDS PARADE
WESTERN
CLIFF RD.
98
1
2
3
4
5
6
62

TN21
Well Shaw
Leabridge Farm
Hopgarden Shaw
NORTH STREET
VICARAGE
Lea Bridge
Hill Harbour
Boggy Wood
Parsonage Barn
THE GRANARY RURAL BUS. CEN.
A267
CHURCH LA.
Stone House Farm
LANE
River
Broad Farm
MILL
CHURCH PTH.
The Vicarage
Cuckmere
Trail
Nursery
ROAD STATION
Hall
CHURCH
Hellingly
Hellingly Primary School
Horselunges
Station House
Moat
Cemy.
War Mem.
B2104
Nursery
Woods Corner
White House
Cuckoo
Lower Horsebridge
STREET
Nursery
A271
THE WILLOWS
BAKERS FARM PARK HOMES
Longfields
Horselunges Wood
Upper Horselunges Farm
Brook House
Knights Farm
UPPER
Pav.
Rec.Grd.
Bowl. Grn.
Horse Bridge
Mill
Upper Horsebridge
HORSEBRIDGE ROAD
A22
BOSHIP RBT.
Factory
Hotel
Mill Bri.
OLD MILL CL.
LONDON
MANOR
MANOR PARK CL.
PARK ROAD
LANSDOWNE WY.
LANSDOWNE CR.
LANSDOWNE RD.
LANS-DOWNE GDS.
DRIVE
UNION CL.
Prim. Sch.
Play. Fld.
HAWKS FARM CL.
QUINNELL DR.
HOWLETT DR.
ANGLESEY AV.
LUNDY WLK.
ROCKALL DR.
THE PADDOCKS
ASHBURNHAM PL.
STROMA GDNS.
SOLWAY
ARRAN CL.
MEDWAY
FARNE CL.
FAIRISLE CL.
MORAY WY.
BEXLEY CL.
DOUGLAS CL.
HAWTHYLANDS
Air Strip
River
GOODWIN CL.
AVENUE
CROMER
LEAP CROSS SMALL BUS. CEN.
Welbury Farm
PORTLAND CL.
LOWLANDS
MILLAND RD.
FARMERS
FERN GRN.
JASMINE GRN.
ACORN GRN.
BLOSSOM
OLDFIELD
ILEX GRN.
MILLAND
HEMPSTEAD
GLENEAGLES
GREENFIELDS
LANE
Woodside Farm
Cuckmere
Hempstead Farm
Grovelands Prim. Sch.
Resource Cen.
DERWENT CL.
Playing Field
THE CEDARS
Ten. Cts.
Hailsham Comm. Coll.
Chicheley Farm (Caravan Site)
Tile Hurst
WOBURN
DUNBAR DR.
LAVENDER
HOLYHEAD
DRIVE
GROVELANDS RD.
ROAD
PITREAVIE DR.
CAMERON
Grovelands Farm
Tilehurst
Tile Hurst

6

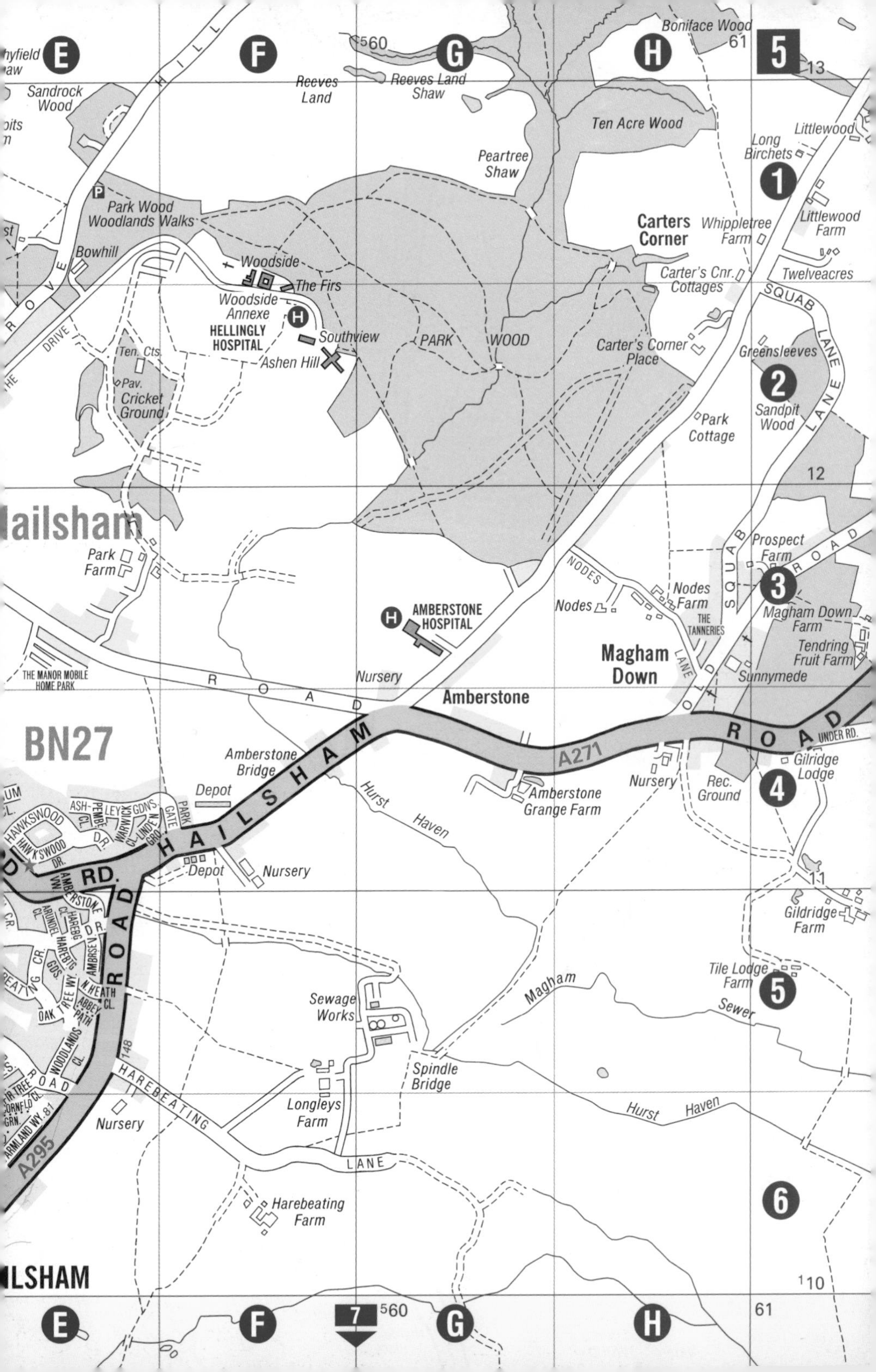

5
E
F
G
H
Boniface Wood
Reeves Land
Reeves Land Shaw
Sandrock Wood
Ten Acre Wood
Long Birchets
Littlewood
Peartree Shaw
Park Wood Woodlands Walks
Carters Corner
Whippletree Farm
Littlewood Farm
Bowhill
Woodside
The Firs
Carter's Cnr. Cottages
Twelveacres
Woodside Annexe
HELLINGLY HOSPITAL
Southview
Ashen Hill
PARK
WOOD
Carter's Corner Place
Greensleeves
SQUAB LANE
Sandpit Wood
Ten. Cts.
Pav.
Cricket Ground
Park Cottage
Hailsham
Park Farm
Prospect Farm
NODES
Nodes Farm
Nodes
AMBERSTONE HOSPITAL
Magham Down Farm
Tendring Fruit Farm
THE TANNERIES
Magham Down
Sunnymede
THE MANOR MOBILE HOME PARK
ROAD
Nursery
Amberstone
BN27
HAILSHAM ROAD
A271
UNDER RD.
Gilridge Lodge
Amberstone Bridge
Depot
Nursery
Rec. Ground
Amberstone Grange Farm
Hurst Haven
HAWKSWOOD
RD.
Gildridge Farm
Sewage Works
Magham Sewer
Tile Lodge Farm
Spindle Bridge
Longleys Farm
Hurst Haven
HAREBEATING LANE
Nursery
A295
Harebeating Farm
LSHAM
7
560
61

Chicheley Farm (Caravan Site)
Tile Hurst
Resource Cen.
Prim. Sch.
Playing Field
Hailsham Comm. Coll.
LONDON ROAD
B2104
GROVELANDS RD.
DERWENT CL.
CEDARS
WOBURN CL.
DUNBAR DR.
GLENEAGLES
HOLYHEAD CL.
PITREAVIE DR.
Grovelands Farm
CAMERON
CL.
ST. BOSWELLS CL.
ST. MELLION CL.
MELROSE CL.
FOREST VIEW
TILE-HURST DR.
SUMMERFIELDS
SUMMER CT.
ROPE WK.
SILVERDALE CT.
BEUZEVILLE
SUMMERHEATH RD.
HAWKINS
WOODPECKER DR.
MOUNTAIN ASH CL.
WESTERN RD.
Tilehurst Farm
Tile Hurst
Sub.
TROON COTTS.
A22
TURNBERRY DR.
DRIVE
BUSHEY FIELDS
HAMELSHAM CT.
SUSSEX AV.
SUSSEX CL.
GREEN GRO.
THE BELFRY
MAPLE CT.
CHERRY SIDE
THE DIPLOCKS
ASH CT.
Diplocks Farm
THE HAWTHORNS
PINE WY.
BRAMBLE DR.
ROAD
WESTERN RD.
TENNIS
Lib.
Recreation Ground
NORTH CRESCENT IND. EST.
HAILSHAM INDUSTRIAL PK.
DIPLOCKS WAY
AVOCET
DAWBER BLDGS.
CROFT WKS.
Knock Hatch Cottage
HEMPSTEAD LANE
Falconry Centre
Knock Hatch Farm
Knockhatch Adventure Park
Dry Ski Slope
Bushy Wood (Scout Camp)
Bushy Wood Farm
APEX WAY
THE MARTLETS
CROWN CL.
DIPLOCKS BLDGS.
THE SQ.
APEX PARK
BURFIELD PARK INDUSTRIAL ESTATE
A295
GORDON RD.
ORCHARD
PALMERS RW.
KNIGHTS GDN.
WINDSOR RD.
FACTORY LANE
09 Ruffet's Wood
ARLINGTON ROAD WEST
Hidgate Cott.
Arlington Stadium (Speedway)
Highlands Farm Cottages
Highlands Farm
COOPERS
CARPENTERS WY.
MILLERS RISE
THE HOLT
SOUTH CL.
SOUTH ROAD
B2104
ERSHAM WY.
NURSERY
MEADOW RD.
ARLINGTON ROAD EAST
FENS
DITCHLING WY.
DITCHLING WAY
CABURN WY.
CACKLE BURY CL.
OAKLANDS WY.
QUINTIN CL.
INGRAMS WAY
INGRAMS WY.
SANDBANKS CL.
SANDBANKS GRO.
SANDBANKS
THE SHERWOOD GRN.
THE GROVE
Ersham Farm
GILBERT
Cemetery
Robin Post
ROBINS POST LA.
THE GLADE
POLEGATE RD.
Highlands Wood
ARLINGTON EAGLES ROUNDABOUT
Oaklands
ERSHAM ROAD
Robin Post Wood
Bolney's Farm
Gillridge Wood
WILMINGTON WOOD
POST LANE
Bolney's Wood
08
Ersham House
Coldthorn Wood
Folkington Wood
WOODSIDE WAY
ROBINS POST LANE
COLDTHORNE LANE
Woodside Hall
Tudor Close
Summer Hill
Depot
Natewood Farm
Brownings
Coppards
Mulbrook Farm
Gate Wood
SUMMER HILL
Natewood Poultry Farm
BN26
07
PEEL HOUSE FARM CARAVAN PARK
Peel House
Cliff Coom
Depot
Nightingale Place
ROBINS
NATE WOOD
57
58
A
B
C
D
1
2
3
4
5
6

4
8

E
F
5
560
G
H
61
110
WHELPLEY LEVEL
HAILSHAM
Lagoon Leisure Centre
Marshfoot Farm
Seaforth Farm
MARSHFOOT LANE
Old Marshfoot Farm
Marshlands Prim. Sch.
Playing Field
EAST LA.
AVENUE
GREENACRES DR.
NURSERY CL.
VICARAGE FIELD
VICARAGE RD.
TIMBERS CT.
CHAPEL
BARN C.
MKT.
MKT. SQ.
HIGH STREET
GREENWICH RD.
DACRE PK.
NEWTON PK.
VEGA CL.
ORION CL.
CAPELLA PATH
OBSERVATORY
PHOENIX CL.
TEAL CT.
ANTARES PATH
THE GAGES
Cattle Mkt.
MARKET ST.
THE STILES
ST. MARY'S
CLYDE PK.
MOORE PK.
GEERING PK.
HALLEY PK.
HOLLAMBY PK.
MORTAIN PK.
OTHAM PK.
GEMMA CL.
MERLIN CT.
OBSERVATORY VW.
SOUTHERDEN CL.
STONEY LA.
ELMSDOWN PL.
ASHFORD
ELIZABETH CT.
BANKS RD.
MILL
BAYHAM ROAD
FLETCHER CL.
THE STRINGWALK
BOWLEY ROAD
THE ACORNS
ARCHERY
Little Marshfoot Farm
Mill Farm
Lion House
LION HOUSE PARK
SACKVILLE RD.
NEW BARN CL.
THE LAWNS
PELHAM CRES.
WALK
SWAN ROAD
HOWARD CL.
BUTTSFIELD
STATION ROAD INDUSTRIAL ESTATE
WHITE DYKE ROAD
Lookers Cottage
SNAPSON'S DROVE
White Dyke Farm
Castle Cottage
White Dyke
09
SWAN BARN BUS. CEN.
Factory
OLD SWAN LANE
SWAN BARN CARAVAN SITE
New Barn Farm
Sewage Works
Hailsham
BN27
Horse Eye Sewer
08
Westdown Cottages
Downash Farm
Slyes Farm
Slyes Farm Cottages
Nursery
Downash
Falkenvil
Downash Manor Farm
Down Oak
Gassons Farm
Westfield Farm
SALTMARSH LANE
West Downs
Seymours Farm
Little Downash Farm
Pond
Saltmarsh
The Lewen's
Lugear Farm
Honeycrock
Sewer
GLYNLEIGH
LEVEL
07
Holm
9
560
61
Boat
1
2
3
4
5
6

8
6
14
Gate Wood
Natewood Farm
Natewood Poultry Farm
Brownings
Coppards
Mulbrooks Farm
NATE WOOD
Cophall Wood
Ogg's Wood
Cliff Coombe
Depot
Nightingale Place
Nightingale Villas
Nightingale Farm
Rosebank
The Old Thatched Cottage
Nightingale Cottage
Willow Cottage
Woodlands Cottage
Oldfield House
Sayerlands
Sayerland
Bramley Farm
Otham Court
Cuckoo Trail
POLEGATE
BAY TREE LA.
BAY TREE LANE LINK
SAYERLAND LANE
OTHAM
POLEGATE
A22
A27
POLEGATE BY-PASS
HAILSHAM ROAD
Polegate Prim. School
Lib.
STATION ROAD
Polegate Honey Farm
Depot
LEWES ROAD
A27
Polegate
THE CENTRE
EASTBOURNE ROAD
A2270
HYPERION AVENUE
SUNSTAR LANE
GOLDEN MILLER LA.
THE STUD FARM STABLES
The Rough
FOLKINGTON LANE
Recreation Ground
Weir
Playing Field
Playing Fields
Wannock Coppice
SOUTHFIELD
WANNOCK DRIVE
Tower mill
Willows Farm
Pav.
Peel House

BN27
GLYNLEIGH LEVEL
Holmmarsh Bridge
B2104
Morland
Glynleigh Farm
Boat House
Glyndley Manor Hotel
GLYNDLEY MANOR COTTAGE ESTATE
Warren Plantation
Heatherdene
West Lodge
Decoy Wood
East Lodge
Glynleigh Sewer
Drockmill
Marland Bridge
Marland
Pit (disused)
New Barn Farmhouse
New Barn Farm
New Barn Cottage
Glynleigh Cottage
COTTAGE LA.
Old Court Cotts.
Priesthawes Farm
Lower Priesthawes Cottages
Priesthawes
Polegate
Little Friars Farm
BN26
Puddle
Duck
Pevensey
HAILSHAM ROAD
SHEPHAM LANE
Shepham Wood
The Pines
BN24
Drockmill Hill Gut
A27
Little Shepham
BY-PASS
Sharnfold Cottages
Greenacres
Sharnfold Farm
Blackness
PEVENSEY A27 BY-PASS
CHURCH CL.
GLYNLEIGH DR.
FAIROAKS
DROCKMILL CL.
LEVETT CL.
Ditton's Corner
Winfield Farm
DITTONS ROAD
ABERDALE RD.
MARY'S
BRAMLEY RD.
RUSSET CL.
BLENHEIM CL.
Depot
Works
CHAUCER INDUSTRIAL ESTATE
Sewage Works
Dittons
DITTONS
B2247
The Dell
BARN CL.
RED DYKE COTTAGES
HAMBLE RD.
ARUN
Hankham Place
DARWELL DR.
MEDWAY LA.
HANKHAM CT.
BEAULIEU
DARENT CL.
AV.
STOUR CL.
ROTHER CL.
CHERWELL CL.
KENNET CL.
Mill Ditch
GOLDEN JUBILEE WAY
A22
Willingdon & West Langney Sewer
Eastbourne
BN22
Stream
Willingdon
BROAD OAK CL.
STONEGATE
LAUGHTON
CABURN CL.
MOLE CL.
SWALE CL.
LAMBOURN
WELLSBOURNE
07
06
105
04
560
61
7
10
15
E F G H
1 2 3 4 5 6

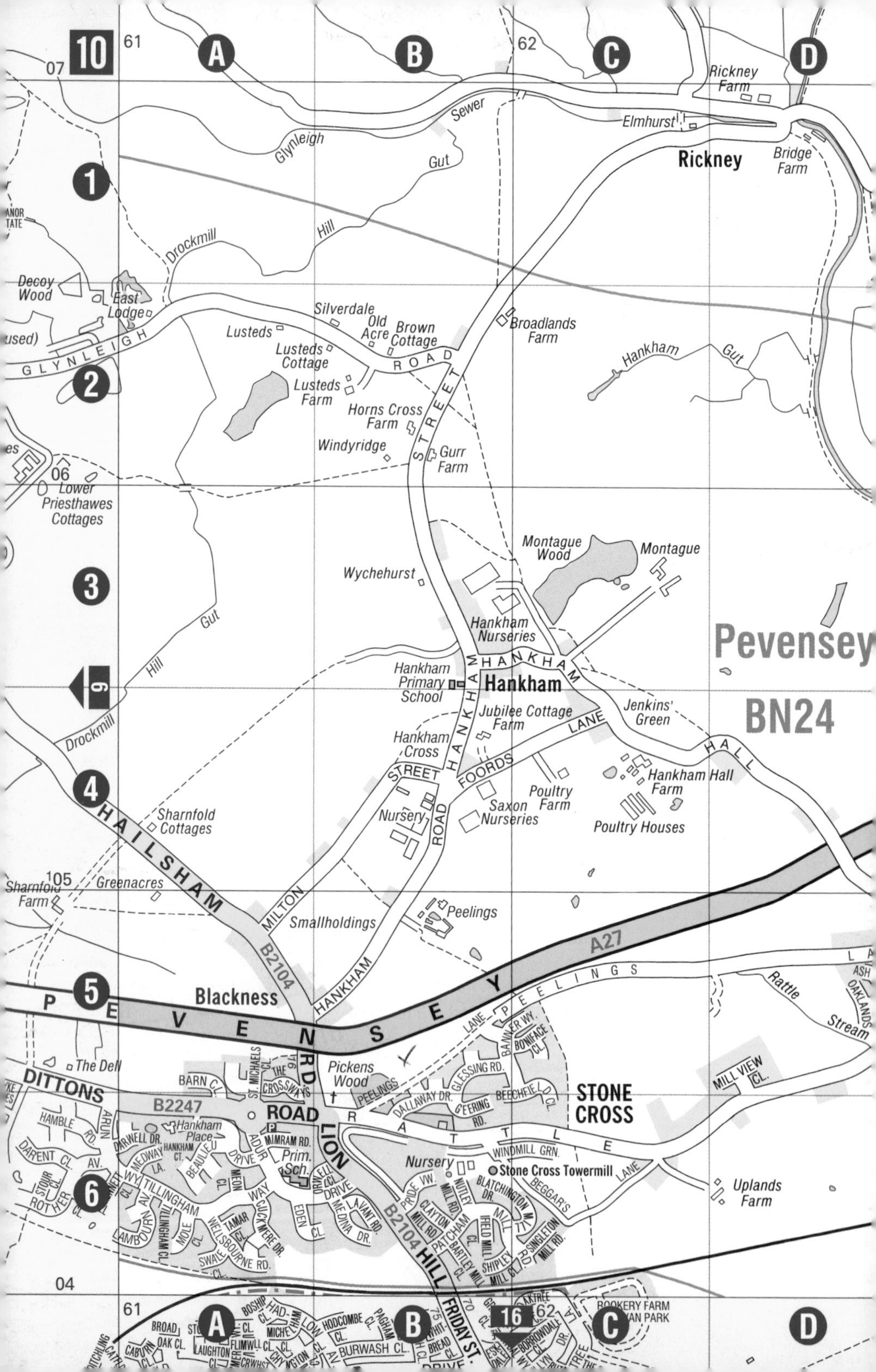

Rickney Farm
Elmhurst
Rickney
Bridge Farm
Sewer
Glynleigh
Gut
Hill
Drockmill
Decoy Wood
East Lodge
GLYNLEIGH ROAD
Silverdale
Old Acre
Brown Cottage
Lusteds
Lusteds Cottage
Lusteds Farm
Horns Cross Farm
Windyridge
Gurr Farm
STREET
Broadlands Farm
Hankham Gut
Lower Priesthawes Cottages
Montague Wood
Montague
Wychehurst
Hankham Nurseries
Pevensey
BN24
Hankham Primary School
Hankham
HANKHAM
Jubilee Cottage Farm
Jenkins' Green
Hankham Cross
HANKHAM STREET
FOORDS LANE
HALL
Hankham Hall Farm
Poultry Farm
Saxon Nurseries
Poultry Houses
Nursery
ROAD
Sharnfold Cottages
HAILSHAM
Greenacres
Sharnfold Farm
MILTON
Smallholdings
Peelings
A27
B2104
PEVENSEY
Blackness
PEELINGS
Rattle Stream
The Dell
DITTONS
Pickens Wood
BANNER WY.
BONIFACE CL.
GLESSING RD.
BEECHFIELD CL.
STONE CROSS
MILL VIEW CL.
B2247
ROAD
LION
RATTLE
DALLAWAY DR.
GEERING RD.
Hankham Place
MIMRAM RD.
Prim. Sch.
WINDMILL GRN.
Stone Cross Towermill
BEGGAR'S LANE
Uplands Farm
HAMBLE RD.
ARUN
DARENT CL.
AV.
STOUR CL.
ROTHER
MEDWAY LA.
HANKHAM CT.
BEAULIEU
ADUR DRIVE
MEON CL.
WAY
TILLINGHAM
TILLINGHAM CL.
LAMBOURN AV.
MOLE CL.
WELLSBOURNE RD.
TAMAR CL.
CUCKMERE DR.
EDEN CL.
ORWELL CL.
DRIVE
MEDINA DR.
LAVANT RD.
SWALE CL.
PRIDE VW.
CLAYTON MILL RD.
MILL RD.
NUTLEY
BLATCHINGTON MILL DR.
PATCHAM MILL RD.
BARTLEY MILL
FIELD MILL
SHIPLEY MILL CL.
SINGLETON MILL RD.
HILL
FRIDAY ST.
BOOKERY FARM
BROAD OAK CL.
LAUGHTON CL.
FLIMWELL CL.
MICHELHAM
HODCOMBE CL.
PAGHAM CL.
BURWASH CL.
BORROWDALE
16
07 06 105 04 61 62
A B C D
1 2 3 4 5 6
9

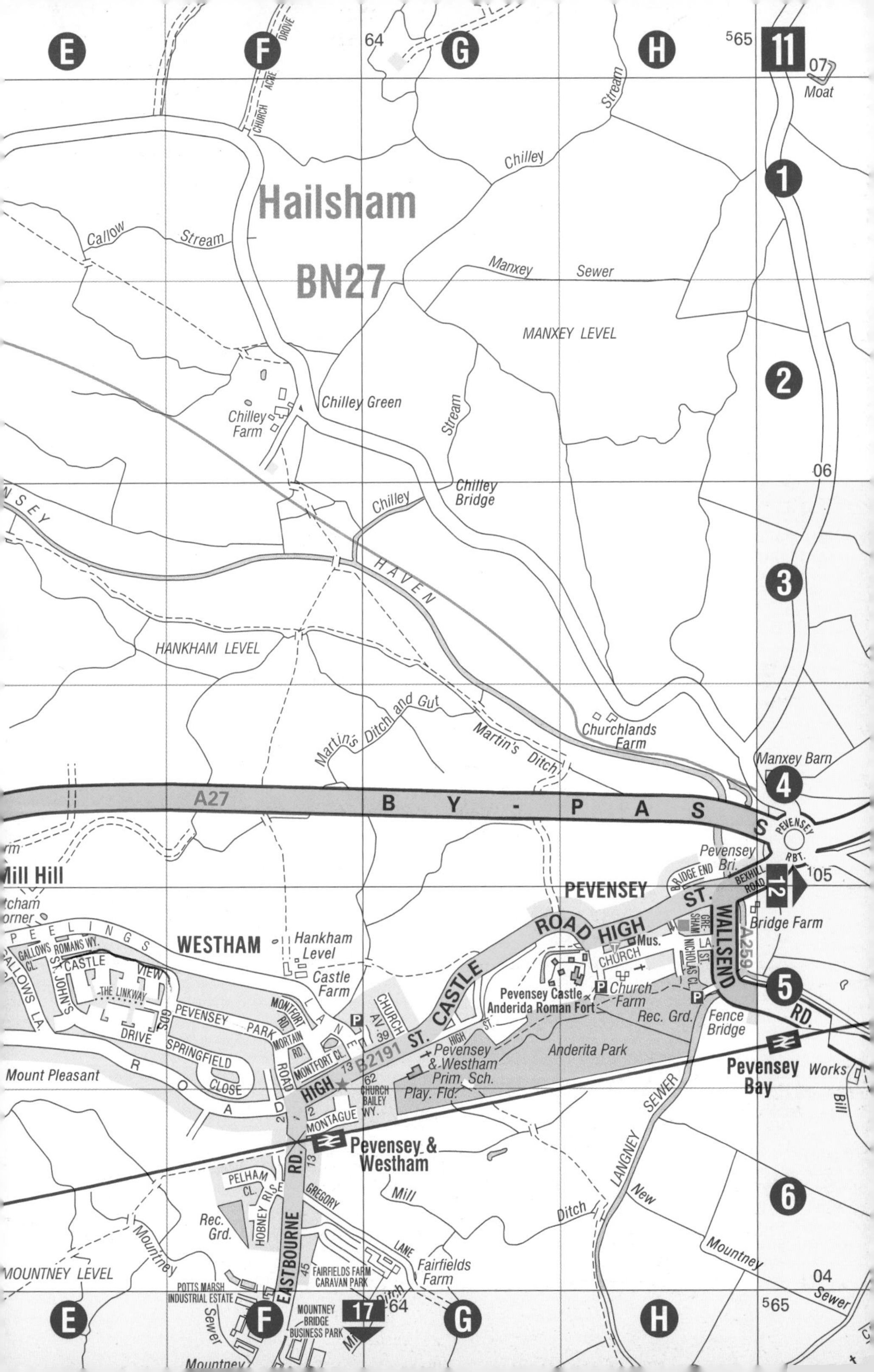
E
F
G
H
564
565
07
Moat
CHURCH ACRE DROVE
Stream
Chilley
Hailsham
BN27
Callow
Stream
Manxey
Sewer
MANXEY LEVEL
1
2
3
4
5
6
Chilley Green
Chilley Farm
Stream
Chilley Bridge
Chilley
06
PEVENSEY
HAVEN
HANKHAM LEVEL
Martin's Ditch and Gut
Martin's Ditch
Churchlands Farm
Manxey Barn
A27
BY-PASS
PEVENSEY RBT.
Pevensey Bri.
BRIDGE END
BEXHILL ROAD
12
105
Bridge Farm
Mill Hill
PEVENSEY
HIGH ST.
ROAD
HIGH
CASTLE ST.
WALLSEND
A259
GRESHAM
LA.
NICHOLAS CL.
Mus.
CHURCH
Pevensey Castle
Anderida Roman Fort
Church Farm
Rec. Grd.
Fence Bridge
RD.
PEELINGS
WESTHAM
Hankham Level
Castle Farm
GALLOWS CL.
ROMANS WY.
ST. JOHN'S
CASTLE VIEW
THE LINKWAY
GALLOWS LA.
PEVENSEY PARK ROAD
DRIVE
SPRINGFIELD CLOSE
MONTFORT RD.
MORTAIN RD.
MONTFORT CL.
LANE
CHURCH AV.
39
B2191
HIGH ST.
Pevensey & Westham Prim. Sch.
Anderita Park
Pevensey Bay
Works
Bill
Mount Pleasant
HIGH
62
CHURCH BAILEY WY.
MONTAGUE WY.
Play. Fld.
LANGNEY SEWER
Pevensey & Westham
PELHAM CL.
HOBNEY RISE
GREGORY LANE
EASTBOURNE RD.
Mill
Ditch
New
Mountney
Rec. Grd.
Mountney
MOUNTNEY LEVEL
45
FAIRFIELDS FARM CARAVAN PARK
Fairfields Farm
POTTS MARSH INDUSTRIAL ESTATE
Sewer
MOUNTNEY BRIDGE BUSINESS PARK
17
64
Ditch
04
Sewer
Mountney

Hailsham
BN27
Pevensey
BN24
A259
Old Haven
Manxey Barn
PEVENSEY BY-PASS
PEVENSEY RBT.
BEXHILL ROAD
BRIDGE END
HIGH ST.
WALLS-END
Pevensey Bri.
Bridge Farm
PEVENSEY
Fence Bridge
Rec. Grd.
Pevensey Bay
Works
SALT HAVEN
PEVENSEY BRIDGE LEVEL
Hall
BEACHLANDS
PEVENSEY BAY
ROAD
RICHMOND RD.
EASTBOURNE ROAD
Martello Tower no.60
Martello Tower no.61
PEVENSEY BAY
New Mountney Sewer
Gut
Bill
EASTBOURNE
MARTELLO BEACH CARAVAN PARK
GREY TOWER ROAD
GREY TOWER CARAVAN SITE
Martello Tower no.62
GREY TOWERS BUNGALOWS
Outfall
Depot
MARESFIELD
SUNSET CL.
ARUNDEL CL.
MOUNTNEY DR.
THE SQUARE
THE BOULEVARD
WESTHAM DR.
CAMBER
MARINE AV.
SOUTH CL.
BROOKLAND CL.
COAST
PEBBLE RD.
COBALD RD.
PARADE
BAY AV.
SEAVILLE DR.
WAVERLEY GDNS.
PRIORY CL.
Lib.
CASTLE DRIVE
CASTLE DR.
NORTH RD.
WESTERN RD.
BAY RD.
COLLIER RD.
WARMINSTER RD.
SEA RD.
THE PROMENADE
LEYLAND RD.
ROSETTI RD.
NORMAN RD.
CASTLERS RD.
VAL PRINSEPS RD.
INNINGS DRIVE
BEACHINGS
CADOGAN CT.
GRENVILLE RD.
TIMBERLAINE
MILLWARD RD.
CLARENCE CT.
RAGLAN CT.
A B C D
1 2 3 4 5 6
11
17
565
66
06
04
03

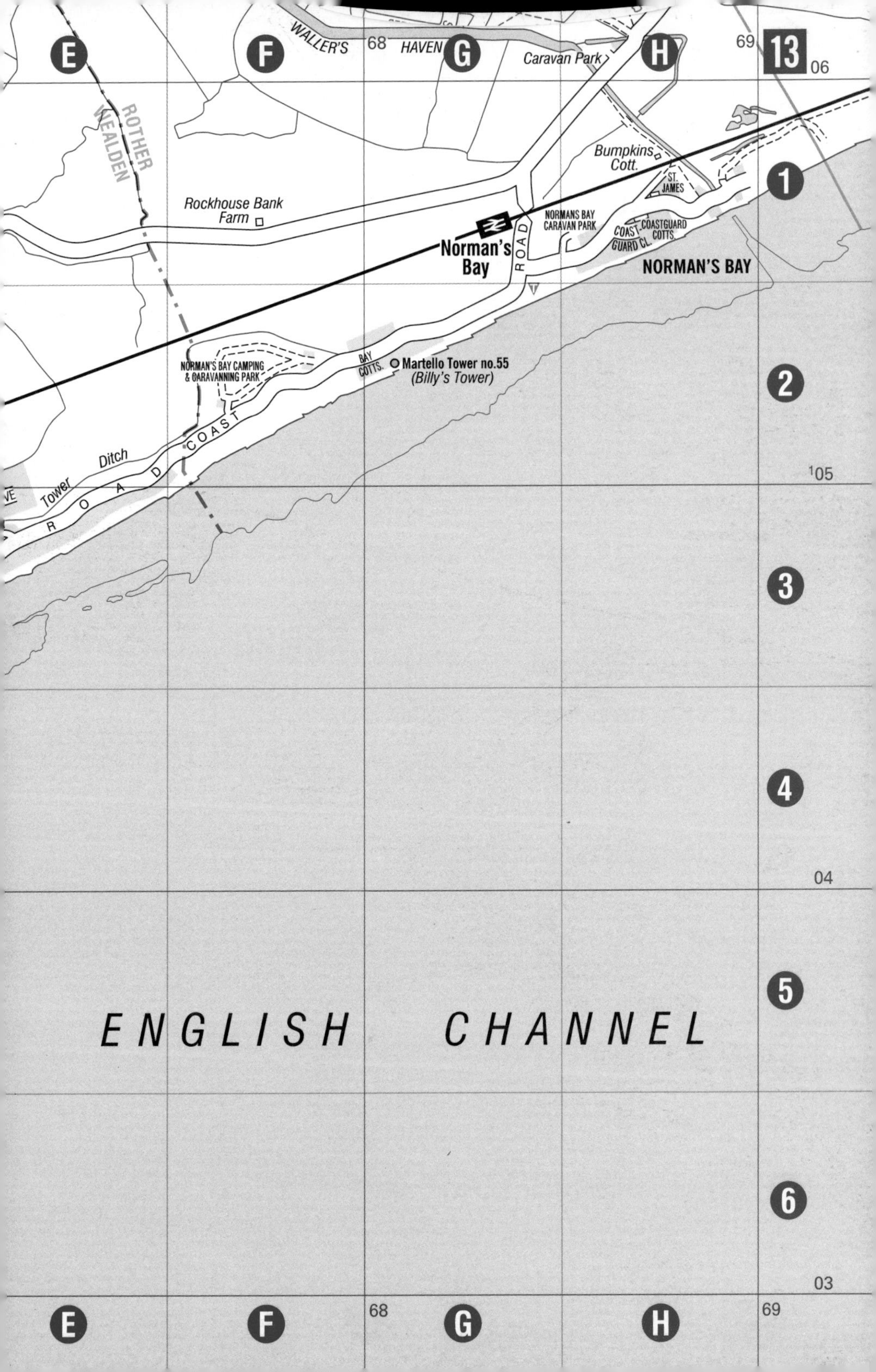

13
E
F
G
H
WALLER'S
68
HAVEN
Caravan Park
69
06
ROTHER
WEALDEN
Bumpkins
Cott.
ST. JAMES
Rockhouse Bank
Farm
NORMANS BAY
CARAVAN PARK
COASTGUARD
COTTS.
COAST GUARD CL.
Norman's
Bay
ROAD
NORMAN'S BAY
1
NORMAN'S BAY CAMPING
& CARAVANNING PARK
BAY
COTTS.
Martello Tower no.55
(Billy's Tower)
2
COAST
Ditch
Tower
ROAD
105
3
4
04
5
ENGLISH CHANNEL
6
03
68
69

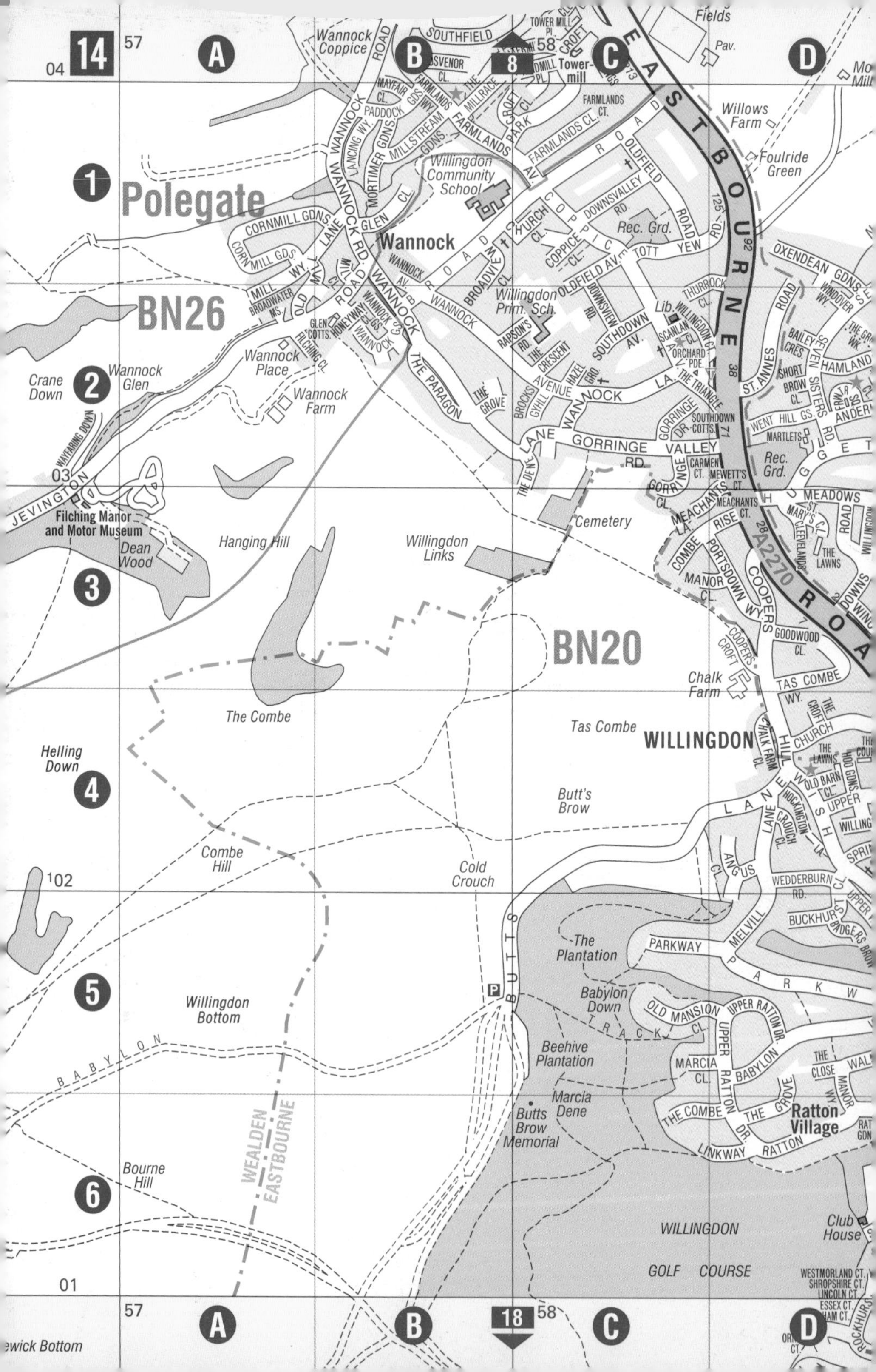

14
57
58
04
03
102
01
A
B
C
D
1
2
3
4
5
6
8
18
Polegate
BN26
BN20
Wannock
WILLINGDON
Ratton Village
Wannock Coppice
Wannock Glen
Wannock Place
Wannock Farm
Crane Down
Filching Manor and Motor Museum
Dean Wood
Hanging Hill
Willingdon Links
Cemetery
The Combe
Tas Combe
Chalk Farm
Helling Down
Butt's Brow
Combe Hill
Cold Crouch
Willingdon Bottom
Bourne Hill
The Plantation
Babylon Down
Beehive Plantation
Marcia Dene
Butts Brow Memorial
WILLINGDON GOLF COURSE
Club House
Willows Farm
Foulride Green
Fields
Pav.
Tower-mill
Willingdon Community School
Willingdon Prim. Sch.
Rec. Grd.
Lib.
WEALDEN
EASTBOURNE
EASTBOURNE ROAD
A2270
JEVINGTON
WAYFARING DOWN
BABYLON
TRACK
SOUTHFIELD
FARMLANDS
FARMLANDS CL.
FARMLANDS CT.
FARMLANDS AV.
MILLRACE
MILLSTREAM GDNS.
MORTIMER GDNS.
LANCING WY.
PADDOCK GDNS.
MAYFAIR CL.
CROFT PARK
TOWER MILL PL.
WANNOCK ROAD
WANNOCK LANE
WANNOCK RD.
WANNOCK AV.
WANNOCK LA.
WANNOCK GDNS.
GLEN CL.
CORNMILL GDNS.
MILL WY.
MILL RD.
BROADWATER MS.
OLD MILL LA.
GLEN COTTS.
FILCHING CL.
HONEYWAY CL.
THE PARAGON
THE GROVE
OLDFIELD ROAD
OLDFIELD AV.
COPPICE AV.
COPPICE CL.
CHURCH CL.
BROADVIEW CL.
DOWNSVALLEY RD.
DOWNSVIEW RD.
TOTT YEW RD.
RAPSON'S RD.
THE CRESCENT
SOUTHDOWN AV.
HAZEL GRO.
AVENUE
BROCKS GYHLL
THE DENE
GORRINGE VALLEY RD.
GORRINGE DR.
GORRINGE CL.
CARMEN CT.
MEWETT'S CT.
MEACHANTS LA.
MEACHANTS CT.
SOUTHDOWN COTTS.
THE TRIANGLE
ORCHARD PDE.
SCANLAN CL.
WILLINGDON CT.
THURROCK CL.
COMBE RISE
PORTSDOWN WY.
MANOR CL.
COOPERS WY.
COOPERS CROFT
GOODWOOD CL.
TAS COMBE WY.
THE CROFT
CHURCH
CHALK FARM CL.
HILL
LANE
WISH HILL
THE LAWNS
OLD BARN CL.
HOCKINGTON LA.
CROUCH LANE
CROUCH CL.
UPPER
ANGUS CL.
WEDDERBURN RD.
MELVILL
BUCKHURST CL.
PARKWAY
OLD MANSION CL.
UPPER RATTON DR.
MARCIA CL.
BABYLON
THE GROVE
THE COMBE
RATTON DR.
LINKWAY
RATTON
THE CLOSE
MANOR WY.
BUTTS
OXENDEAN GDNS.
WINDOVER WY.
ROAD
BAILEY CRES.
SEVEN SISTERS RD.
ST. ANNES
SHORT BROW CL.
HAMLANDS
WENT HILL GS.
MARTLETS
MEADOWS ROAD
ST. MARY'S CL.
CLEVELANDS
THE LAWNS
DOWNS
WESTMORLAND CT.
SHROPSHIRE CT.
LINCOLN CT.
ESSEX CT.
ewick Bottom

E
F
G
H
9
560
61
04
Willingdon & West Langney Sewer
Willingdon
Upper
Stream
GOLDEN
A22
JUBILEE
WAY
Shinewater Lake
1
2
3
4
5
6
03
02
01
LOWER WILLINGDON
BN22
BN21
Eastbourne
SISTERS
HAZELWOOD AVENUE
MALVERN
WOBURN WY.
KIRKSTALL CL.
TINTERN CL.
FOUNTAINS CL.
ROSEDALE PL.
CROXDEN
ROWAN AV.
WALSINGHAM CL.
Comm. Cen.
Oakwood Sch.
Hampden Park Inf. Sch.
MAYWOOD AVENUE
ACACIA ROAD
BRODRICK ROAD
Eastbourne Tech. Coll.
The Lindfield School
Hampden Pk. Sports Cen.
Parkland Jun. & Inf. Schs.
Decoy Wood
HAMPDEN PARK
Decoy Pond
War Mem.
Ham Shaw
Elm Grove Smallholdings
David Lloyd Leisure
Trax Indoor Karting Cen.
Superstore
Lloyds Lane
Hampden Park
Hampden
Park
Lib.
Health Cen.
Rec. Grd.
Percival
Tennis Courts
Bowl. Grn.
Indoor Bowling Club
Rugby Pitch
Pavs.
Playing Fields
Rugby Club
Eastbourne Sports Park
Running Track
Grandstand
Playing Field
Sussex Downs College
Ratton School
The Coppice
EASTBOURNE DISTRICT GENERAL HOSPITAL
KING'S DR.
KING'S DRIVE
A2021
WILLINGDON ROAD
A2270
CROSS LEVELS WAY
A2280
BROADWATER RDBT.
DECOY RDBT.
WILLINGDON RDBT.
MOUNTFIELD RDBT.
HAMPDEN PK. IND. EST.
HAMPDEN RETAIL PK.
BRAMPTON RD. TRAD. EST.
LOTTBRIDGE DROVE
DALLINGTON ROAD
WILLINGDON LANE
STREET
FRISTON AVENUE
PARKFIELD AVENUE
BRASSEY AVENUE
ROSEBERY AV.
DECOY DRIVE
HAMPDEN PARK DRIVE
WESTWOOD AV.
WOODLAND AV.
LINDFIELD
PULBOROUGH AVENUE
FREEMAN AVENUE
KINGSTON ROAD
SACKVILLE RD.
BROADWATER WY.
EASTBOURNE G
Southbourne Lake
SOUTHBO
Sewer
Pit (dis.)
Ocklynge Jun. Sch.
19
16

16
A
B
C
D
10
1
2
3
4
5
6
ROOKERY FARM CARAVAN PARK
Friday Street Farm
FRIDAY STREET
FRIDAY STREET
LARKSPUR DRIVE
MILFOIL DRIVE
SORREL DRIVE
PENNINE WY.
Hazel Court Sch. & The Causeway Nursery Sch.
Shinewater Lake
Prim. Sch.
Hlth. Cen.
Comm. Cen.
Play. Fld.
GOLDEN JUBILEE WAY
A22
B2104
B2191
DROVE
HIDE
LANGNEY
WILLINGDON DROVE
SEVENOAKS
Langney Shop. Cen.
LANGNEY
BN22
Hydneye Bridge
Shinewater Rbt.
Health Club
Factory
WILLINGDON LEVELS
WEST LANGNEY LEVEL
Eastbourne
Langney Sewer
Willingdon & West Langney Sewer
BN23
HIGHFIELD LINK
A2280
Lottbridge Rbt.
LOTTBRIDGE DROVE
A2290
CROSS LEVELS WAY
Hampden Park
Hampden Retail Pk.
Hampden Pk. Ind. Est.
Highfield Ind. Est.
Marshall Roundabout
Mountfield Roundabout
Playing Field
Superstore
Brampton Rd. Trad. Est.
Driving Range
Club House
Lott Bridge
EASTBOURNE GOLFING PARK
WILLINGDON LEVEL
Eastbourne Miniature Steam Railway Adventure Park
Southbourne Lake
SOUTHBOURNE LEVEL
ST. ANTHONY'S HILL
Bus Depot
Hawthorn Rd. Ind. Est.
Birch Industrial Estate
Hammonds Ind. Est.
Depot
Gas Storage Station
Finmere Rd. Ind. Est.
Birch Rbt.
Seaside Rbt.
SEASIDE
Playing Field
Jun. Sch.
Compton Ind. Est.
Eastbourne Crematorium
Rec. Grd.
School
15
20
61
62
04
03
02
01

17
Pevensey
BN24
Sovereign Harbour
Langney Village
ENGLISH CHANNEL
EASTBOURNE ROAD
PEVENSEY BAY ROAD
HIDE HOLLOW
Mountney Bridge
MOUNTNEY LEVEL
EAST LANGNEY LEVEL
Langney East Sports Club
Eastbourne Borough FC (Priory Lane Stadium)
SOVEREIGN HARBOUR RETAIL PARK
UGC Cinema
Sovereign Harbour Marina
Inner Harbour
Outer Harbour
Lifeboat Station
Locks
Breakwater
Martello Tower no.64
Martello Tower no. 66
Martello Tower
Langney Point Outfall
MARTELLO BEACH CARAVAN PARK
BAY VIEW CAMPING AND CARAVANNING PARK
CASTLE VIEW CARAVAN AND CAMPING SITE
CANNON CAMPING PARK
MOUNTNEY BRIDGE BUSINESS PARK
POTTS MARSH INDUSTRIAL ESTATE
FAIRFIELD CARAVAN PARK
The German's
11
12
21

18
14
22
WEALDEN
EASTBOURNE
WILLINGDON
GOLF COURSE
Further Plantation
Foxholes Brow
Foxholes
Resr. (covered)
Duttle's Brow
Willingdon Hill
Eldon Bottom
BN20
The Peak
Crunden's Bottom
Beachy Brow
EASTBOURNE DOWNS
GOLF COURSE
Ringwood
Chapman's
Bottom
Pea Down
Bottom
Ringwood
New Barn
Club House
Cherry Garden Plantation
Youth Hostel
Pashley Down Inf. Sch.
The Downs Sch.
Citadel
Old Te Rec.
PASHLEY
EAST DEAN
WARREN HILL
A259
B2103
Crapham Hill
Halfway Cottages
Crapham Barn
Crapham Bottom

E
F
G
H
15
19
Playing Field
EASTBOURNE DISTRICT GENERAL HOSPITAL
Hosp. Accom.
KING'S
WAY
LEVELS
A2280
CROSS
RODMILL RBT.
BN22
1
Lottbridge
EASTBOURNE LEVEL
Upperton Farm
Sewer
SOUTHBOU
Lake
Poultry
2
St. Thomas a Becket Cath. Jun. & Inf. Schs.
WILLINGDON
A2021
DRIVE
KINGS CL.
PRIDEAUX ROAD
LEWES RD.
GORRINGE
TUTTS BARN LA.
100
Depot
MAYFIELD
BEDFORDWELL ROAD
3
ROBOROUGH DAY HOSP.
UPPER AV.
20
Pit (dis.)
Ocklynge Jun. Sch
STUART AV.
COBBOLD
BEVERINGTON RD.
WESTFIELD
SELSFIELD CL.
TOVEY CL.
ERIDGE
TWINEHAM RD.
SELMESTON
RANGEMORE DRIVE
BURTON RD.
POCOCK'S RD.
CLAXTON CL.
PARKER CL.
FENNELL'S CL.
RUTLAND CL.
VIELDINGS CL.
WINDMILL CL.
AVENUE
The Cavendish School
Cavendish Sports Centre
A2270
ELDON ROAD
LONG ACRE CL.
MACMILLAN DR.
BN21
DAVID HEIGHTS
ROSSINGTON CL.
KING'S
PRIDEAUX
ASHBURNHAM GDS.
BRUN
ROAD
OLD TOWN
Motcombe Inf. Sch.
Cemetery
MILL RD.
UPPERTON
CAREW
UPPERTON ROAD
SELWYN
MILTON
MILTON CRES.
SHORTDEAN PL.
MOUNTNEY RD.
GORE PARK RD.
CHARLESTON RD.
BIRLING ST.
MONCEUX RD.
DILLINGBURGH
MOTCOMBE
GREEN
Pool
ST. MARY'S RD.
Uni.
TORFIELD
ARUNDEL
EVERSFIELD
Hartfield Sq.
THE AVENUE
EASTBOURNE
4
TERMINUS RD.
GILDREDGE RD.
CHURCH ST.
HIGH ST.
THE GOFFS
ROAD
A259
Towner Art Gall. & Local Mus.
Mnr. Gds.
Bowl. Grns.
Gildredge Park
SOUTHFIELDS
ARLINGTON
SAFFRONS
UPWICK RD.
DACRE
VICARAGE
SUMMERDOWN
GREYS RD.
YMCA
SUMMERDOWN COURT
Temple Grove
Sports Grd.
COMPTON COURT
COMPTON LODGE
Law Cts.
The Saffrons
Town Hall
Lib.
SOUTH ST.
5
SOUTH STREET
Eastbourne
CAMP
War. Meml. Fld.
DRIVE
Club House
PARADISE
PARADISE DRIVE
Playing Fld.
ROYAL EASTBOURNE GOLF COURSE
EASTBOURNE
Compton Place
Compton Park
FURNESS
GRANGE GDNS.
GRASSINGTON
COLLEGE
Coll.
Eastbourne College
Fitness Cen.
Ten. Cen.
Devonshire Park
Theatres
BLACKWATER
GRANVILLE
CARLISLE
Tennis Courts
Trevin Towers
University of Brighton (Welkin Site)
Bernersmede
SAFFRONS
MEADS
6
JEVINGTON
KING EDWARDS PARADE
Paradise Plantation
Reservoir (covered)
Moira House Schools
Univ. of Brighton (Hillbrow)
DRIVE
Warren
Playing
23
98
560
61

20
16
19
3
A
B
C
D
1
2
3
4
5
6
SOUTHBOURNE LEVEL
EASTBOURNE LEVEL
Lottbridge
Sewer
Upperton Farm
Poultry Farm
St. Thomas Becket Cath. Jun. & Inf. Sch.
Stafford Jun. Sch.
ROSELANDS
BN22
Eastbourne
Roselands Infant Sch.
Works
Depot
Superstore
FINMERE RD. IND. EST.
BRITLAND ESTATE
Hlth. Cen.
The Oval
Crumbles Pond
Princes Park
Bowl Grns.
Musgrave Collection
Ten. Cts.
Lifeboat Station
Lifeboat Launching Ramp
Treasure Island Adventure Park
Bowl. Grns.
Redoubt Fortress The Military Mus. of Sussex
GLENNYS IND. EST.
Rec. Grd.
THE LAWNS
ROBOROUGH DAY HOSP.
EAST BOURNE
ARNDALE CEN.
Cin.
Syn.
Thtre.
Sch.
Pier
EASTBOURNE
BN21
HOSP.
Ten. Cen.
Fitness Cen.
Eastbourne College
Devonshire Park Theatres
Bandstand
Lifeboat Museum
Martello Tower no.73 The Wish Tower Puppet Museum
Western Lawns
A2021
A259
B2103
2103
NORTHBOURNE ROAD
SOUTHBOURNE ROAD
RINGWOOD ROAD
WHITLEY ROAD
SEASIDE
ROYAL PDE.
MARINE PDE.
MARINE PARADE
GRAND PARADE
KING EDWARDS PARADE
PROMENADE
LOWER PROMENADE
SEASIDE RD.
TERMINUS RD.
TRINITY TREES
SOUTH ST.
DEVONSHIRE PL.
ASHFORD RD.
ST. LEONARDS RD.
UPPER AV.
THE AVENUE
LEWES RD.
GILDREDGE RD.
CARLISLE ROAD
COMPTON ST.
CAVENDISH PL.
LANGNEY RD.
BEACH RD.
SEAFORD RD.
CHANNEL VIEW ROAD
LOTTBRIDGE DROVE
WOODGATE ROAD
BRIDGEMERE ROAD
CHURCHDALE AV.
SIDLEY RD.
PEVENSEY RD.
61
62
98
99
100

E
F
G
H
17
BN23
PRINCES
ROAD
JERVIS
COLLINGWOOD CL.
WENTWORTH CT.
RANELAGH CT.
FROBISHER CL.
MOUNTBATTEN DR.
JELLICOE CL.
RAMSAY
WAY
SCHOFIELD
KEITH
ROYAL SOVGN
CABOT CL.
PARADE
Works
PROMENADE
Langney Point
Outfall
BLAKES
WAY
WILLIAM
PRINCE
Sovereign Park
PROMENADE
Sovereign Centre
MONARCH HO.
SOVEREIGN RDBT.
COCHRANE CL.
FOLEY CL.
BEATTY
BENBOW AV.
COOK AV.
NELSON DR.
ENGLISH
CHANNEL
1
2
3
4
5
6
565
01
100
099
98
64
E
F
G
H
565

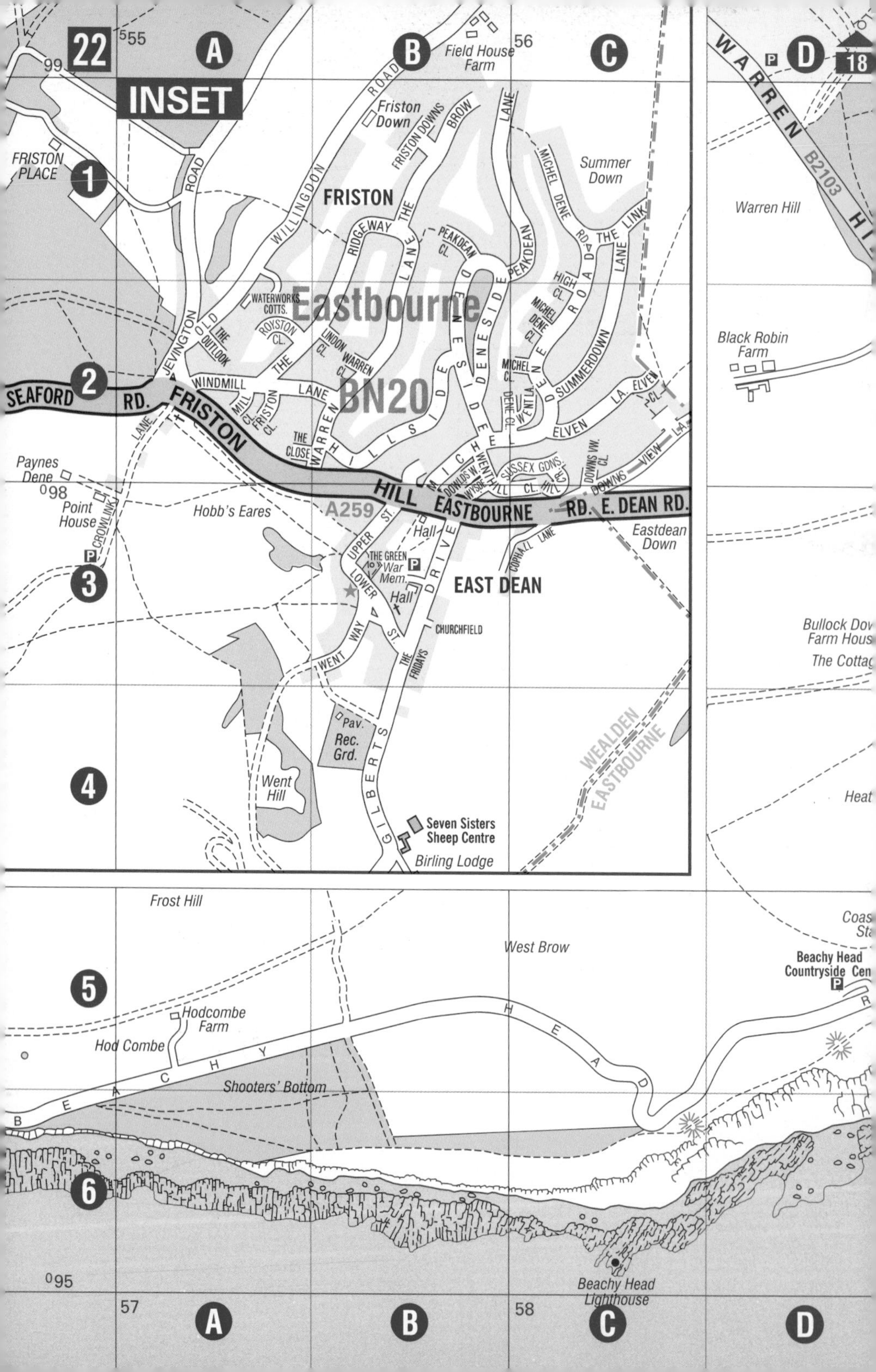
22
INSET
18
FRISTON PLACE
FRISTON
Eastbourne
BN20
EAST DEAN
Field House Farm
Friston Down
Summer Down
Warren Hill
WARREN HILL
B2103
Black Robin Farm
SEAFORD RD.
FRISTON HILL
EASTBOURNE RD.
E. DEAN RD.
A259
Paynes Dene
Point House
Hobb's Eares
Eastdean Down
Bullock Dov Farm Hous
The Cottag
WEALDEN
EASTBOURNE
Went Hill
Rec. Grd.
Pav.
Seven Sisters Sheep Centre
Birling Lodge
Frost Hill
West Brow
Hodcombe Farm
Hod Combe
Shooters' Bottom
BEACHY HEAD
Beachy Head Countryside Cen
Coas Sta
Beachy Head Lighthouse
Heat
CHURCHFIELD
THE FRIDAYS
GILBERTS DRIVE
UPPER ST.
LOWER ST.
WENT WAY
THE GREEN
War Mem.
Hall
COPHALL LANE
JEVINGTON ROAD
WILLINGDON ROAD
OLD JEVINGTON
WINDMILL LANE
WATERWORKS COTTS.
ROYSTON CL.
THE OUTLOOK
MILL CL.
FRISTON CL.
THE CLOSE
WARREN LANE
LINDON CL.
WARREN
HILLSIDE
RIDGEWAY
THE LANE
FRISTON DOWNS
BROW
PEAKDEAN CL.
PEAKDEAN LANE
DENESIDE
MICHEL DENE RD.
THE LINK
HIGH CL.
MICHEL DENE CL.
MICHEL CL.
DENE CL.
WENT LA.
SUMMERDOWN
ELVEN LA.
ELVEN CL.
DOWNS VIEW LA.
DOWNS VW. CL.
SUSSEX GDNS.
WENTHILL
DOWLDS W.
WYSSE
HILL CR.
CROWLINK
LANE
55
56
57
58
99
98
95
A
B
C
D
1
2
3
4
5
6

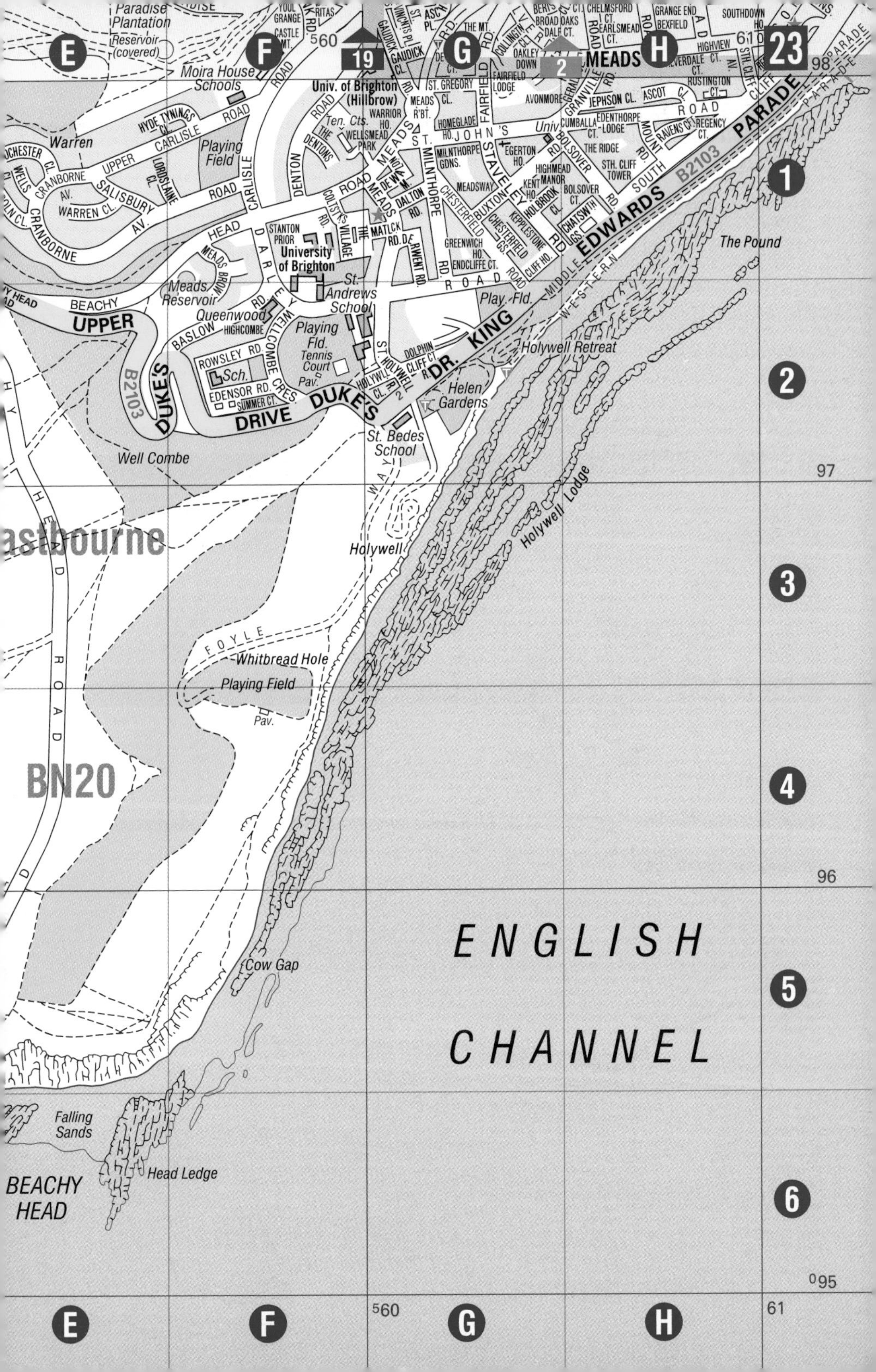

E
F
G
H
19
2
23
MEADS
1
2
3
4
5
6
560
61
98
97
96
95
Paradise Plantation
Reservoir (covered)
Moira House Schools
Warren
Playing Field
Univ. of Brighton (Hillbrow)
University of Brighton
Meads Reservoir
Queenwood
St. Andrews School
Playing Fld.
Tennis Court
Pav.
Sch.
Play. Fld.
Holywell Retreat
Helen Gardens
St. Bedes School
The Pound
Well Combe
Holywell
Holywell Lodge
astbourne
Whitbread Hole
Playing Field
BN20
Cow Gap
ENGLISH
CHANNEL
Falling Sands
Head Ledge
BEACHY HEAD
UPPER CARLISLE ROAD
CARLISLE ROAD
SALISBURY AV.
CRANBORNE AV.
WARREN CL.
DENTON ROAD
MEADS ROAD
ST. JOHN'S ROAD
MILNTHORPE ROAD
STAVELEY RD.
CHESTERFIELD ROAD
DARLEY ROAD
UPPER DUKE'S DRIVE
DUKE'S DRIVE
DR. KING EDWARDS PARADE
SOUTH CLIFF
B2103
BEACHY HEAD ROAD
FOYLE WAY

INDEX

Including Streets, Places & Areas, Hospitals & Hospices, Industrial Estates, Selected Flats & Walkways, Stations and Selected Places of Interest.

HOW TO USE THIS INDEX

1. Each street name is followed by its Postcode District and then by its Locality abbreviation(s) and then by its map reference; e.g. **Abbey Rd.** BN20: Eastb . . . .2D **18** is in the BN20 Postcode District and the Eastbourne Locality and is to be found in square 2D on page **18**. The page number is shown in bold type.

2. A strict alphabetical order is followed in which Av., Rd., St., etc. (though abbreviated) are read in full and as part of the street name; e.g. **Ash Gro.** appears after **Ashgate Rd.** but before **Ashington Rd.**

3. Streets and a selection of flats and walkways too small to be shown on the maps, appear in the index with the thoroughfare to which it is connected shown in brackets; e.g. **Alastair Ct.** *BN21: Eastb . . . .6D **2** (off Compton St.)*

4. Addresses that are in more than one part are referred to as not continuous.

5. Places and areas are shown in the index in **BLUE TYPE** and the map reference is to the actual map square in which the town centre or area is located and not to the place name shown on the map; e.g. **EASTBOURNE . . . .4A 20 (2F 3)**

6. An example of a selected place of interest is **Anderida Roman Fort 5G 11**

7. An example of a station is **Eastbourne Station (Rail) . . . .4A 20 (2E 3)**

8. An example of a hospital or hospice is **AMBERSTONE HOSPITAL 2G 23**

9. Map references shown in brackets; e.g **Alciston M.** BN21: Eastb . . . .5A **20** (3F **3**) refer to entries that also appear on the large scale pages **2-3**.

GENERAL ABBREVIATIONS

App. : Approach
Av. : Avenue
Bri. : Bridge
Bldgs. : Buildings
Bungs. : Bungalows
Bus. : Business
Cvn. : Caravan
Cen. : Centre
Cl. : Close
Cott. : Cottage
Cotts. : Cottages
Ct. : Court
Cres. : Crescent
Cft. : Croft
Dr. : Drive
E. : East
Est. : Estate
Fld. : Field
Gdn. : Garden
Gdns. : Gardens
Ga. : Gate
Gt. : Great
Grn. : Green
Gro. : Grove
Hgts. : Heights
Ho. : House
Ind. : Industrial
Info. : Information
La. : Lane
Mnr. : Manor
Mans. : Mansions
M. : Mews
Mt. : Mount
Mus. : Museum
Nth. : North
No. : Number
Pde. : Parade
Pk. : Park
Pl. : Place
Ri. : Rise
Rd. : Road
Rdbt. : Roundabout
Shop. : Shopping
Sth. : South
Sq. : Square
St. : Street
Ter. : Terrace
Twr. : Tower
Trad. : Trading
Up. : Upper
Vw. : View
Vs. : Villas
Wlk. : Walk
W. : West
Yd. : Yard

LOCALITY ABBREVIATIONS

B'wck : **Berwick**
Down : **Downash**
E Dean : **East Dean**
Eastb : **Eastbourne**
Filch : **Filching**
Folk : **Folkington**
Fris : **Friston**
Hails : **Hailsham**
Hank : **Hankham**
Hell : **Hellingly**
Herst : **Herstmonceux**
Jev : **Jevington**
Lang : **Langney**
Lwr D : **Lower Dicker**
Mag D : **Magham Down**
Milt S : **Milton Street**
Nor B : **Norman's Bay**
Pev : **Pevensey**
Pev B : **Pevensey Bay**
Pole : **Polegate**
Rick : **Rickney**
Sto C : **Stone Cross**
Wart : **Wartling**
W'ham : **Westham**
Will : **Willingdon**
Wilm : **Wilmington**

A

E

Earlsmead Ct.
BN20: Eastb 6H **19** (6C **2**)
EASTBOURNE . . . . **4A 20 (2F 3)**
Eastbourne All Saints Church
Brass Rubbings Cen. *2F 3*
(off Susan's Rd.)
Eastbourne Arndale Cen.
BN21: Eastb 4A **20** (2E **3**)
Eastbourne Av. BN24: Pev B 4B **12**
Eastbourne Bandstand . . .5B 20 (4G 3)
Eastbourne Borough FC
(Priory Lane Stadium) 2F 17
Eastbourne College
Pennell Ho. *4D 2*
(off College Rd.)
Eastbourne Crematorium
BN23: Lang 2D **16**
Eastbourne Deluxe Bingo Club
. . . . *2F 3*
(off Pevensey Rd.)
EASTBOURNE DISTRICT
GENERAL HOSPITAL 1G 19
Eastbourne Heritage Cen. *5F 3*
(off Carlisle Rd.)
Eastbourne Lifeboat Mus.
. . . . .6A 20 (5F 3)
Eastbourne Local History Mus.
. . . . .4F 19 (1A 2)
Eastbourne Miniature Steam Railway
Adventure Pk. 6A 16
Eastbourne Pier 5B 20 (3H 3)
Eastbourne Rd.
BN20: E Dean 3B **22**
BN20: Will 1C **14**
BN24: Pev B 3H **17**
BN24: W'ham 1F **17**
BN26: Pole, Will 5B **8**
Eastbourne Sports Pk. 5G 15
Eastbourne Station (Rail)
. . . . **4A 20 (2E 3)**
East Cl. BN26: Pole 5D **8**
EAST DEAN **3B 22**
E. Dean Rd. BN20: Eastb 3C **22**
Eastern Av. BN26: Pole 4D **8**
E. Well Pl. BN27: Hails 1D **6**
Eaton Ct. BN21: Eastb 3H **19**
Ecmod Rd. BN22: Eastb 1C **20**
Eden Cl. BN24: Sto C 6A **10**
Edensor Rd. BN20: Eastb 2F **23**
Edenthorpe Lodge
BN20: Eastb 1H **23**
Edgeland Ter. BN22: Eastb 4H **15**
Edinburgh Ct. *BN20: Eastb* *2E* ***19***
(off Central Av.)
Edison Rd. BN23: Eastb 4A **16**
Edmund Cl. BN23: Eastb 5E **17**
Edward Rd. BN22: Eastb 4A **16**
Egbert Cl. BN23: Eastb 5E **17**
Egerton Ho. BN20: Eastb 1G **23**
Elderwood Cl. BN22: Eastb 3F **15**
Eldon Rd. BN21: Eastb 2E **19**
Elgar Way BN23: Lang 2E **17**
Elizabeth Ct. BN20: Eastb 2E **19**
BN26: Pole 5C **8**
BN27: Hails 2E **7**
Elm Ct. *BN26: Pole* *5C* ***8***
(off Walnut Wlk.)
Elm Grn. BN27: Hails 6D **4**
Elm Gro. BN22: Eastb 4H **15**
Elms Av. BN21: Eastb 5B **20** (3G **3**)
Elmsdown Pl. BN27: Hails 2E **7**
Elms Rd. BN21: Eastb 5B **20** (3G **3**)
Elmwood *BN21: Eastb* *3H* ***19***
(off Arundel Rd.)
Elmwood Cl. BN23: Lang 1C **16**
Elmwood Gdns. BN23: Lang 1C **16**
Elsted Cl. BN22: Eastb 3A **16**
Elven Cl. BN20: E Dean 2C **22**
Elven La. BN20: E Dean 2C **22**
Embassy Ct. BN21: Eastb 2H **19**
Endcliffe Ct. BN20: Eastb 1G **23**
Ensenada Reef BN23: Eastb 4H **17**
Enterprise Shop. Cen.
BN21: Eastb *2D* ***2***
(off Wharf Rd.)
Enys Ct. BN21: Eastb 3H **19**
Enys Rd. BN21: Eastb 4H **19** (1C **2**)
Erica Cl. BN23: Lang 3B **16**
Eridge Rd. BN21: Eastb 6E **15**
Ersham Rd. BN27: Hails 4D **6**
Ersham Way BN27: Hails 3D **6**
Eshton Rd. BN22: Eastb 2C **20**
Eskdale Cl. BN23: Lang 1B **16**
ESPERANCE BMI HOSPITAL, THE
. . . . .5A 20 (3F 3)
Essex Ct. BN20: Eastb 1D **18**
Etchingham Rd. BN23: Lang 4E **17**
Ethelred Cl. BN23: Eastb 5E **17**
Eton M. BN21: Eastb 4A **20** (1E **3**)
Eugene Way BN23: Eastb 4H **17**
Eversfield Ct. BN21: Eastb 1D **2**
Eversfield Ho. BN21: Eastb 1D **2**
Eversfield Rd. BN21: Eastb 3H **19**
Eversley Ct. BN21: Eastb 3G **19**
Exceat Cl. BN23: Lang 1A **16**
Exeter Cl. BN22: Will 3D **14**

F

Factory La. BN27: Hails 2B **6**
Fairfield Lodge
BN20: Eastb 6G **19** (6B **2**)
Fairfield Rd.
BN20: Eastb 1G **23** (6B **2**)
Fairfields Farm Cvn. Pk.
BN24: W'ham 6F **11**
Fair Isle Cl. BN23: Eastb 5E **17**
Fairisle Cl. BN27: Hails 5C **4**
Fairlight Ct. BN26: Pole 5C **8**
Fairlight Rd. BN22: Eastb 2C **20**
Fairoaks BN26: Pole 5E **9**
Fairway Cl. BN20: Eastb 5E **19**
Falcon Way BN27: Hails 4D **4**
Falmer Cl. BN20: Eastb 6D **14**
BN22: Eastb 4F **15**
Falmouth Cl. BN23: Eastb 5F **17**
Faraday Cl. BN22: Eastb 4H **15**
Farlaine Rd. BN21: Eastb 6E **15**
Farmlands Av. BN26: Pole 1B **14**
Farmlands Cl. BN26: Pole 1C **14**
Farmlands Ct. BN26: Pole 1C **14**
Farmlands Way BN26: Pole 6B **8**
Farmland Way BN27: Hails 6E **5**
Farne Cl. BN27: Hails 5B **4**
Farnol Ho. BN21: Eastb 3F **19**
Farrington Ct.
BN21: Eastb 4H **19** (2C **2**)
Fastnet Cl. BN23: Eastb 5E **17**
Faversham Rd. BN23: Lang 3D **16**
Faygate Rd. BN22: Eastb 3G **15**
Fennell's Cl. BN21: Eastb 2G **19**
Fern Cl. BN23: Lang 2C **16**
Fern Grn. BN27: Hails 6D **4**
Fidley Cl. BN23: Eastb 6E **17**
Fieldings, The BN21: Eastb 3H **19**
Fife Ct. BN22: Eastb 3A **16**
FILCHING **3A 14**
Filching Cl. BN26: Pole 2A **14**
Filching Ct. BN20: Eastb 2D **18**
Filching Manor & Motor Mus.
. . . . .3A 14
Filching Rd. BN20: Eastb 2D **18**
Filder Cl. BN22: Eastb 1A **20**
(not continuous)
Finistere Av. BN23: Eastb 5E **17**
Finmere Cl. BN22: Eastb 1C **20**
Finmere Ct. BN22: Eastb 1C **20**
Finmere Rd. BN22: Eastb 1C **20**
Finmere Rd. Ind. Est.
BN22: Eastb 6C **16**
Firle Rd. BN22: Eastb 3B **20**
Fir Tree Cl. BN27: Hails 6E **5**
Firwood Cl. BN22: Eastb 4G **15**
Fisher Cl. BN23: Eastb 6F **17**
Fitzalan Ho. *BN21: Eastb* *3H* ***19***
(off Arundel Rd.)
Fitzgerald Cl. BN20: Eastb 6C **2**
Fitzmaurice Av. BN22: Eastb 2B **20**
Fleming Cl. BN23: Lang 3F **17**
Fletcher Cl. BN27: Hails 2E **7**
Fletching Rd. BN22: Eastb 3A **16**
Flimwell Cl. BN23: Lang 1A **16**
Foley Cl. BN23: Eastb 6E **17**
Folkington La. BN26: Folk 6A **8**
Foords La. BN24: Hank 4B **10**
Foredown Cl. BN20: Eastb 5E **19**
Forest Vw. BN27: Hails 1C **6**
Formula Fun Go-Karts
Fort Fun 2E 21
Fort Fun BN22: Eastb 2E **21**
Fort La. BN22: Eastb 1D **20**
Fort Rd. BN22: Eastb 1D **20**
Fountains Cl. BN22: Eastb 2G **15**
Foxglove Rd. BN23: Lang 2B **16**
Foyle Way BN20: Eastb 3F **23**
Framfield Way BN21: Eastb 1F **19**
Fraser Av. BN23: Eastb 6E **17**
Freeland Ho. *BN20: Eastb* *6C* ***2***
(off Silverdale Rd.)
Freeman Av. BN22: Eastb 4G **15**
Frenchgate Cl. BN22: Eastb 3H **15**
Frenchgate Rd. BN22: Eastb 3H **15**
Freshfield Cl. BN27: Hails 3D **6**
Freshford Cl. BN23: Lang 3D **16**
Freshwater Sq. BN22: Will 2D **14**
Freshway, The BN22: Eastb 2E **15**
Fridays, The BN20: E Dean 3B **22**
FRIDAY STREET **1C 16**
Friday St. BN23: Lang 1B **16**
FRISTON **1B 22**
Friston Av. BN22: Will 4E **15**
Friston Cl. BN20: Fris 2A **22**
Friston Downs BN20: Fris 1B **22**
Friston Hill
BN20: E Dean, Fris 2A **22**
Friston Ho. BN21: Eastb 3G **19**
Frobisher Cl. BN23: Eastb 6E **17**
Fulbourne Ho.
BN20: Eastb 6G **19** (5B **2**)
Furness Cl. *BN21: Eastb* *3D* ***2***
(off South St.)
Furness Rd.
BN20: Eastb 5H **19** (4C **2**)
BN21: Eastb 5H **19** (4D **2**)

G

Gables Ct.
BN21: Eastb 3A **20** (1E **3**)
Gages, The BN27: Hails 2F **7**
Gainsborough Cres.
BN23: Lang 4D **16**
Gainsborough La. BN26: Pole 5A **8**
Gallows Cl. BN24: W'ham 5E **11**
Gallows La. BN24: W'ham 5E **11**
Galveston Cl. BN23: Eastb 6F **17**
Gannet Ho.
BN21: Eastb 5A **20** (3F **3**)
Garden Ct. *BN21: Eastb* *4F* ***3***
(off Devonshire Pl.)
Gardner Cl. BN23: Eastb 6E **17**
Garfield Rd. BN27: Hails 2E **7**
Garnet Dr. BN20: Will 6E **15**
Gaudick Cl.
BN20: Eastb 6G **19** (6A **2**)
Gaudick Rd.
BN20: Eastb 6F **19** (5A **2**)
Geering Pk. BN27: Hails 2F **7**
Geering Rd. BN24: Sto C 6B **10**
Gemma Cl. BN27: Hails 2G **7**
George St. BN27: Hails 2E **7**
Gilbert Rd. BN22: Eastb 3B **20**
Gilberts Dr. BN20: E Dean 4B **22**
Gilbert Way BN27: Hails 4D **6**
Gilda Cres. BN26: Pole 5C **8**
Gildredge Rd.
BN21: Eastb 4H **19** (2D **2**)
Glade, The BN27: Hails 3B **6**
Gladstone Cl. BN22: Eastb 4H **15**
Gladstone Ct. *BN21: Eastb* *3G* ***3***
(off Terminus Rd.)
Glebe Cl. BN20: Eastb 4F **19**
Glen Cl. BN26: Pole 1B **14**
Glen Cotts. BN26: Pole 2B **14**
Glendale Av. BN21: Eastb 1E **19**
Gleneagles Dr. BN27: Hails 6C **4**
Glenmore M.
BN21: Eastb 4A **20** (1E **3**)
Glennys Ind. Est.
BN22: Eastb 2C **20**
Glenthorne Ho. *BN21: Eastb* *1C* ***2***
(off Arundel Rd.)
Glessing Rd. BN24: Sto C 5B **10**
Gloucester Cl. BN22: Will 3E **15**
Gloucester Ct.
BN20: Eastb 6H **19** (5C **2**)
BN23: Lang 4E **17**
Glynde Av. BN22: Eastb 4G **15**
Glyndley Mnr. Cottage Est.
BN24: Hank 1H **9**
Glynleigh Dr. BN26: Pole 4E **9**
Glynleigh Rd.
BN24: Hails, Hank 1E **9**
Goffs, The
BN21: Eastb 4G **19** (1A **2**)
Golden Ga. Way BN23: Eastb . . .4G **17**
Golden Jubilee Way
BN22: Eastb 1H **15**
BN24: Sto C 5G **9**
Golden Miller La. BN26: Pole 5A **8**
Golding Rd. BN23: Lang 3F **17**
Goldsmith Cl. BN23: Lang 2E **17**
Goodwin Cl. BN27: Hails 5C **4**
Goodwood Cl. BN20: Will 3D **14**
Gordon Ho. *BN21: Eastb* *3H* ***19***
(off Carew Rd.)
Gordon Rd. BN27: Hails 2D **6**
Gore Pk. Av. BN21: Eastb 3F **19**
Gore Pk. Rd. BN21: Eastb 3F **19**
Gorringe Cl. BN20: Will 2C **14**
Gorringe Dr. BN20: Will 2C **14**
Gorringe Rd. BN21: Eastb 2A **20**
BN22: Eastb 2H **19**
Gorringe Valley Rd.
BN20: Will 2C **14**
Gorse Cl. BN20: Eastb 2D **18**
Gosford Way BN26: Pole 5B **8**
Goudhurst Cl. BN23: Lang 4D **16**
Grafton Ct.
BN21: Eastb 4B **20** (2G **3**)
Grampian Cl. BN23: Lang 2C **16**
Granary Rural Bus. Cen., The
BN27: Hell 1B **4**
Grand Ct. BN21: Eastb 6A **20** (5F **3**)
Grand Mans. *BN20: Eastb* *6E* ***3***
(off Silverdale Rd.)
Grand Pde.
BN21: Eastb 6A **20** (5F **3**)
BN26: Pole 5B **8**
Grange, The *BN21: Eastb* *3F* ***3***
(off North St.)
Grange Ct.
BN21: Eastb 5H **19** (4C **2**)
Grange End
BN21: Eastb 6H **19** (6D **2**)
Grange Gdns.
BN20: Eastb 5H **19** (4C **2**)
(Blackwater Rd.)
BN20: Eastb 5H **19** (4C **2**)
(Furness Rd.)
Grange Lodge *BN20: Eastb* *4C* ***2***
(off Grassington Rd.)
Grange M.
BN21: Eastb 5H **19** (3D **2**)
Grange Rd.
BN21: Eastb 5H **19** (3D **2**)
Granville Ct.
BN20: Eastb 6H **19** (5C **2**)
Granville Crest BN20: Eastb 1G **23**
Granville Rd.
BN20: Eastb 5H **19** (4C **2**)
Grasmere Cl. BN23: Lang 1B **16**
Grassington Rd.
BN20: Eastb 5H **19** (4C **2**)
Gt. Cliffe Rd. BN23: Lang 4E **17**
Green, The BN20: E Dean 3B **22**
BN27: Hails 4E **5**
Greenacres Dr. BN27: Hails 1E **7**
Greenacres Way BN27: Hails 1E **7**
Greencroft *BN21: Eastb* *3G* ***3***
(off Trinity Pl.)
Greenfield Rd. BN21: Eastb 3F **19**
Greenfields BN27: Hails 6C **4**
Green Gro. BN27: Hails 1D **6**
Greenleaf Gdns. BN26: Pole 3C **8**
Green St. BN21: Eastb 3E **19**
Green Wlk. BN27: Hails 6E **5**
Green Wlk., The BN22: Will 2D **14**
Greenway BN20: Eastb 1D **18**
Greenwich Ho. BN20: Eastb 1G **23**
Greenwich Rd. BN27: Hails 2F **7**
Gregory La. BN24: W'ham 6F **11**
Grenada Cl. BN23: Eastb 6G **17**
Grenville Rd. BN24: Pev B 5A **12**
Gresham BN24: Pev 5H **11**
Gresham Cl. BN21: Eastb 1E **19**
Greys Rd. BN20: Eastb . . .4F **19** (1A **2**)
Grey Tower Bungs.
BN24: Pev B 6A **12**
Grey Tower Cvn. Site
BN24: Pev B 2H **17**
Grey Tower Rd. BN24: Pev B 2H **17**
Grosvenor Cl. BN26: Pole 6B **8**
Grosvenor Ct. *BN21: Eastb* *3H* ***19***
(off Enys Rd.)
Grosvenor Quay BN23: Eastb . . .5G **17**
Grove, The BN20: Will 6D **14**
(Up. Ratton Dr.)
BN20: Will 2B **14**
(Wannock La.)
BN27: Hails 3D **6**
Grove Hill BN27: Hell 2E **5**
Grovelands Rd. BN27: Hails 6C **4**
Grove Rd.
BN21: Eastb 5H **19** (3C **2**)
Guardian Ct. BN26: Pole 4B **8**
Guestling Rd. BN22: Eastb 2D **20**
Gwent Ct. *BN22: Eastb* *3C* ***20***
(off St James Rd.)

H

Hadley Ct. BN26: Pole 6C **8**
Hadley Ho.
BN21: Eastb 4H **19** (1D **2**)
Hadlow Av. BN23: Lang 1A **16**

I

J

K

L

Leap Cross Small Bus. Cen.
BN27: Hails . . . 6C **4**
Le Brun Rd. BN21: Eastb . . . 2G **19**
Leeds Av. BN23: Eastb . . . 5D **16**
Leeward Quay BN23: Eastb . . . 5F **17**
Leicester Ct. *BN22: Eastb . . . 3B 20*
(off Leslie St.)
Lennox Cl. BN20: Eastb . . . 2D **18**
Lepeland BN27: Hails . . . 6C **4**
Leslie St. BN22: Eastb . . . 3B **20**
Letheren Pl. BN21: Eastb . . . 4F **19**
Levett Av. BN26: Pole . . . 4E **9**
Levett Cl. BN26: Pole . . . 5E **9**
Levett Rd. BN26: Pole . . . 5E **9**
Levett Way BN26: Pole . . . 5E **9**
Lewes Ct. *BN21: Eastb . . . 3H 19*
(off Lewes Rd.)
BN21: Eastb . . . 3A **20**
(Malcolm Ct.)
Lewes Rd. BN21: Eastb . . . 2H **19**
BN26: B'wck, Folk, Milt S,
Pole, Wilm . . . 5A **8**
Leyland Rd. BN24: Pev B . . . 5B **12**
Lilac Cl. BN22: Eastb . . . 3F **15**
Limes, The
BN21: Eastb . . . 3G **19** (1B **2**)
Limetree Av. BN22: Eastb . . . 2F **15**
Lincoln Cl. BN20: Eastb . . . 1E **23**
Lincoln Ct. BN20: Eastb . . . 6D **14**
Linden Cl. BN22: Eastb . . . 2G **15**
Linden Gro. BN27: Hails . . . 4E **5**
Lindfield Dr. BN27: Hails . . . 2D **6**
Lindfield Rd. BN22: Eastb . . . 3F **15**
Lindon Cl. BN20: Fris . . . 2B **22**
Lindsay Cl. BN20: Eastb . . . 5E **19**
Link, The BN20: E Dean . . . 1C **22**
Link Rd. BN20: Eastb . . . 6F **19**
Linkswood
BN21: Eastb . . . 5G **19** (3A **2**)
Linkway BN20: Will . . . 6D **14**
Linkway, The BN24: W'ham . . . 5E **11**
Linnet Cl. BN23: Lang . . . 3C **16**
Linosa Ct. *BN22: Eastb . . . 1H 3*
(off Pevensey Rd.)
Lion Hill BN24: Sto C . . . 6B **10**
Lion Ho. Pk. BN27: Hails . . . 3G **7**
Lion La. BN21: Eastb . . . 4B **20** (2H **3**)
Lismore Rd.
BN21: Eastb . . . 5A **20** (3F **3**)
Lister Rd. BN23: Eastb . . . 4A **16**
Littlecote BN20: Eastb . . . 6H **19** (5C **2**)
Lloyds La. BN22: Eastb . . . 5G **15**
Lodge, The
BN21: Eastb . . . 5A **20** (4E **3**)
Lodge Av. BN22: Will . . . 3E **15**
London Ho. *BN21: Eastb . . . 3E 3*
(off Cornfield Ter.)
London Rd. BN27: Hails . . . 4C **4**
Long Acre Cl. BN21: Eastb . . . 2F **19**
Long Beach Cl. BN23: Eastb . . . 4H **17**
Long Beach M. BN23: Eastb . . . 4H **17**
Long Beach Vw. BN23: Eastb . . . 4H **17**
Longford Ct. BN23: Lang . . . 3D **16**
Longland Rd. BN20: Eastb . . . 3D **18**
Longstone Rd.
BN21: Eastb . . . 4A **20** (2F **3**)
(not continuous)
BN22: Eastb . . . 4B **20** (1G **3**)
Lordslaine Cl. BN20: Eastb . . . 1E **23**
Lothian Ct. BN22: Eastb . . . 3H **15**
Lottbridge Dr. BN22: Eastb . . . 3H **15**
Lottbridge Drove
BN22: Eastb . . . 4H **15**
(not continuous)
BN23: Eastb . . . 4A **16**
Lottbridge Rdbt. BN23: Eastb . . . 5A **16**
Love La. BN20: Eastb . . . 4F **19** (2A **2**)
Lovell Ct. BN21: Eastb . . . 2F **19**
LOWER HORSEBRIDGE . . . 3B **4**
Lower Pde.
BN21: Eastb . . . 6A **20** (5F **3**)
Lower Rd. BN21: Eastb . . . 3F **19**
Lower St. BN20: E Dean . . . 3B **22**
LOWER WILLINGDON . . . 2D **14**
Lowlands, The BN27: Hails . . . 6C **4**
Lowther Cl. BN23: Lang . . . 2D **16**
Loxwood Cl. BN22: Will . . . 5E **15**
Luke Lade Ct. *BN27: Hails . . . 2E 7*
(off Bayham Rd.)
Lullington Cl. BN21: Eastb . . . 6E **15**
Lullington Ho. BN21: Eastb . . . 3G **19**
Lundy Wlk. BN23: Eastb . . . 5F **17**
BN27: Hails . . . 4B **4**
Lushington La.
BN21: Eastb . . . 5A **20** (3E **3**)
Lushington Rd.
BN21: Eastb . . . 5A **20** (3E **3**)
Luton Cl. BN21: Eastb . . . 1E **19**

Lydd Cl. BN23: Lang . . . 3D **16**
Lynholm Rd. BN26: Pole . . . 5D **8**

M

Macmillan Dr. BN21: Eastb . . . 2E **19**
Macquarie Quay BN23: Eastb . . . 5G **17**
Madeira Way BN23: Eastb . . . 5F **17**
Magdalen Cl. BN23: Lang . . . 2C **16**
Magellan Way BN23: Eastb . . . 1G **21**
MAGHAM DOWN . . . 3H **5**
Magnolia Dr. BN22: Eastb . . . 3F **15**
Magnolia Wlk. BN22: Eastb . . . 3F **15**
Magpie Rd. BN23: Lang . . . 2C **16**
Mahwood Ho. *BN21: Eastb . . . 3A 20*
(off Bedfordwell Rd.)
Malcolm Ct. BN21: Eastb . . . 3A **20**
Malcolm Gdns. BN26: Pole . . . 4C **8**
Mallard Cl. BN22: Eastb . . . 4H **15**
Malthouse Cotts. *BN20: Will . . . 4D 14*
(off Wish Hill)
Malvern Cl. BN22: Eastb . . . 2F **15**
Manifold Rd. BN22: Eastb . . . 3B **20**
Manor Cl. BN20: Will . . . 3C **14**
Manor Mobile Home Pk., The
BN27: Hell . . . 3E **5**
Manor Pk. Cl. BN27: Hails . . . 4C **4**
Manor Pk. Ct. BN26: Pole . . . 5C **8**
Manor Pk. Rd. BN27: Hails . . . 4C **4**
Manor Rd. BN22: Eastb . . . 3A **16**
Manor Way BN20: Will . . . 5D **14**
BN26: Pole . . . 5C **8**
Mansions, The BN21: Eastb . . . 5F **3**
Manton Ct. BN23: Eastb . . . 5D **16**
Manvers Rd. BN20: Eastb . . . 4D **18**
Maple Ct. BN27: Hails . . . 1C **6**
Maplehurst Rd. BN22: Eastb . . . 3F **15**
Mapleleaf Gdns. BN26: Pole . . . 3C **8**
Maple Rd. BN23: Eastb . . . 6D **16**
Marcia Cl. BN20: Will . . . 5C **14**
Maresfield Dr. BN24: Pev B . . . 3C **12**
Marina Wlk. BN23: Eastb . . . 5E **17**
Marine Av. BN24: Pev B . . . 3D **12**
Marine Cl. BN24: Pev B . . . 3D **12**
Marine Ct. *BN24: Pev B . . . 4B 12*
(off Terrace, The)
Marine Pde.
BN21: Eastb . . . 5B **20** (3H **3**)
BN22: Eastb . . . 4B **20** (2H **3**)
Marine Rd.
BN22: Eastb . . . 4B **20** (1H **3**)
BN24: Pev B . . . 4B **12**
Marine Ter. BN24: Pev B . . . 4B **12**
Market Pl. BN27: Hails . . . 2E **7**
Market Sq. *BN27: Hails . . . 2E 7*
(off Market St.)
Market St. BN27: Hails . . . 2E **7**
Mark La. BN21: Eastb . . . 5A **20** (3E **3**)
Marlborough Cl. BN23: Lang . . . 2D **16**
Marlborough Ct. *BN21: Eastb . . . 2C 2*
(off Southfields Rd.)
Marlow Av. BN22: Eastb . . . 1B **20**
Marsden Rd. BN23: Lang . . . 4E **17**
Marshall Ct. BN22: Eastb . . . 3F **15**
Marshall Rd. BN22: Eastb . . . 5H **15**
Marshall Rdbt. BN23: Eastb . . . 5A **16**
Marshfoot La. BN27: Hails . . . 1E **7**
Martello Beach Cvn. Pk.
BN24: Pev B . . . 6A **12**
Martello Ct. *BN24: Pev B . . . 6A 12*
(off Grenville Rd.)
Martello Rd. BN22: Eastb . . . 1D **20**
Martello Rdbt. BN23: Eastb . . . 3G **17**
Martello Tower No. 55 . . . 2G **13**
Martello Tower No. 60 . . . 5B **12**
Martello Tower No. 61 . . . 6A **12**
Martello Tower No. 62 . . . 6A **12**
Martello Tower No. 64 . . . 4H **17**
Martello Tower No. 66 . . . 6G **17**
Martello Tower No. 73 . . . 6A **20** (5F **3**)
Martin Ct. BN22: Eastb . . . 3F **15**
Martinique Way BN23: Eastb . . . 6G **17**
Martlets BN22: Will . . . 2D **14**
Martlets, The BN27: Hails . . . 2C **6**
Maryan Ct. BN27: Hails . . . 1D **6**
Matlock Rd. BN20: Eastb . . . 1G **23**
Maxfield Cl. BN20: Eastb . . . 2D **18**
Mayfair Cl. BN26: Pole . . . 1B **14**
Mayfair Ho.
BN21: Eastb . . . 5A **20** (3E **3**)
Mayfield Pl. BN22: Eastb . . . 3A **20**
Mayo Ct. *BN23: Lang . . . 4D 16*
(off Pembury Rd.)
Maywood Av. BN22: Eastb . . . 3F **15**
Meachants Ct. BN20: Will . . . 3D **14**
Meachants La. BN20: Will . . . 3C **14**
Meadhurst BN20: Eastb . . . 6G **19** (5B **2**)

Meadow Cl. BN27: Hails . . . 6D **4**
Meadowlands Av.
BN22: Eastb . . . 3F **15**
Meadow Rd. BN27: Hails . . . 3C **6**
Meadows Rd. BN22: Will . . . 3D **14**
MEADS . . . 1G **23** (6B **2**)
Meads Brow BN20: Eastb . . . 1F **23**
Meads Ct.
BN20: Eastb . . . 6G **19** (5B **2**)
Meads Rd.
BN20: Eastb . . . 1G **23** (6A **2**)
Meads Rdbt.
BN20: Eastb . . . 1G **23** (6A **2**)
Meads St. BN20: Eastb . . . 1G **23**
Meadsway BN20: Eastb . . . 1G **23**
Medina Dr. BN24: Sto C . . . 6B **10**
Medway BN27: Hails . . . 5C **4**
Medway La. BN24: Sto C . . . 6A **10**
Melbourne Rd.
BN22: Eastb . . . 4B **20** (1G **3**)
Melrose Cl. BN27: Hails . . . 1C **6**
Melvill La. BN20: Will . . . 5D **14**
Memorial Rdbt. *BN21: Eastb . . . 3E 3*
(off Cornfield Rd.)
Mendip Av. BN23: Lang . . . 2C **16**
Meon Cl. BN24: Sto C . . . 6A **10**
Merewood Ct. BN21: Eastb . . . 3G **19**
Merlin Ct. BN27: Hails . . . 2G **7**
Merlswood
BN20: Eastb . . . 6G **19** (5B **2**)
Merlynn BN21: Eastb . . . 5A **20** (4F **3**)
Metropole Ct. *BN22: Eastb . . . 1H 3*
(off Royal Pde.)
Mewett's Ct. BN20: Will . . . 2D **14**
Michel Cl. BN20: E Dean . . . 2C **22**
Michel Dene Cl.
BN20: E Dean . . . 2C **22**
Michel Dene Rd.
BN20: E Dean . . . 1C **22**
Michel Gro.
BN21: Eastb . . . 4G **19** (1A **2**)
Michel Gro. Ho.
BN21: Eastb . . . 4G **19** (1B **2**)
Michelham Cl. BN23: Lang . . . 1A **16**
Middleham Way BN23: Lang . . . 1C **16**
Middle Pde.
BN20: Eastb . . . 2G **23** (6E **3**)
BN21: Eastb . . . 6A **20** (6F **3**)
Middlesex Ct. *BN22: Eastb . . . 3B 20*
(off Leslie St.)
Middleton Dr. BN23: Eastb . . . 6E **17**
Midhurst Rd. BN22: Eastb . . . 3H **15**
Milchester Ho. *BN20: Eastb . . . 1G 23*
(off Buxton Rd.)
Milfoil Dr. BN23: Lang . . . 1B **16**
Milland M. *BN27: Hails . . . 6D 4*
(off Milland Rd.)
Milland Rd. BN27: Hails . . . 6D **4**
Millbrook Gdns. BN20: Eastb . . . 1D **18**
Mill Cl. BN20: Fris . . . 2A **22**
BN26: Pole . . . 1B **14**
Millers Ri. BN27: Hails . . . 3C **6**
Millfield Ct.
BN21: Eastb . . . 4G **19** (1C **2**)
Millfields Cl. BN26: Pole . . . 4C **8**
Millfields Ct. BN26: Pole . . . 4C **8**
Mill Gap Rd. BN21: Eastb . . . 3H **19**
MILL HILL . . . 4E **11**
Mill La. BN27: Hell . . . 2C **4**
Millrace, The BN26: Pole . . . 1B **14**
Mill Rd. BN21: Eastb . . . 2F **19**
BN27: Hails . . . 2E **7**
Millstream Gdns. BN26: Pole . . . 1B **14**
Mill Vw. Cl. BN24: W'ham . . . 5D **10**
Millward Rd. BN24: Pev B . . . 6A **12**
Mill Way BN26: Pole . . . 2A **14**
Milnthorpe Gdns.
BN20: Eastb . . . 1G **23**
Milnthorpe Rd. BN20: Eastb . . . 1G **23**
Milton Cres. BN21: Eastb . . . 3E **19**
Milton Grange *BN21: Eastb . . . 3H 19*
(off Arundel Rd.)
Milton Rd. BN21: Eastb . . . 2E **19**
Milton St. BN24: Hank . . . 5A **10**
Mimosa Cl. BN26: Pole . . . 3C **8**
Mimram Rd. BN24: Sto C . . . 6A **10**
Minster Cl. BN26: Pole . . . 4C **8**
Mirasol *BN20: Eastb . . . 6C 2*
(off Silverdale Rd.)
Moat Cft. Ct.
BN21: Eastb . . . 4G **19** (1A **2**)
Moat Cft. Rd.
BN21: Eastb . . . 4G **19** (1A **2**)
Moat Ho. BN21: Eastb . . . 4G **19** (1A **2**)
Mole Cl. BN24: Sto C . . . 6A **10**
Monarch Gdns. BN23: Lang . . . 4F **17**
Monarch Ho. BN22: Eastb . . . 1E **21**
Mona Rd. BN22: Eastb . . . 3B **20**

Monceux Rd. BN21: Eastb . . . 3E **19**
Monk Sherborne Ho.
BN20: Eastb . . . 5C 2
(off Granville Rd.)
Monserrat Vs. BN23: Eastb . . . 6G **17**
Montague Way BN24: W'ham . . . 6F **11**
Montclare Ho. *BN21: Eastb . . . 1B 2*
(off Upperton Rd.)
Montfort Cl. BN24: W'ham . . . 5F **11**
Montfort Rd. BN24: W'ham . . . 5F **11**
Moore Pk. BN27: Hails . . . 2F **7**
Moorings, The *BN20: Eastb . . . 1G 23*
(off St John's Rd.)
Moray Wlk. BN27: Hails . . . 5C **4**
Mortain Pk. BN27: Hails . . . 2F **7**
Mortain Rd. BN24: W'ham . . . 5F **11**
Mortimer Gdns. BN26: Pole . . . 1B **14**
Mortimer Rd. BN22: Eastb . . . 1A **20**
Moss Ho.
BN21: Eastb . . . 5H **19** (3D **2**)
Motcombe La. BN21: Eastb . . . 3F **19**
Motcombe Rd. BN21: Eastb . . . 3F **19**
Motcombe Swimming Pool . . . 3F **19**
Mount, The
BN20: Eastb . . . 6G **19** (6B **2**)
BN27: Hails . . . 3E **7**
Mountain Ash Cl. BN27: Hails . . . 1C **6**
Mountbatten Dr. BN23: Eastb . . . 6E **17**
Mountfield Rd. BN22: Eastb . . . 4H **15**
Mountfield Rdbt. BN22: Eastb . . . 4H **15**
Mountney Bri. Bus. Pk.
BN24: W'ham . . . 1F **17**
Mountney Dr. BN24: Pev B . . . 3D **12**
Mountney Rd. BN21: Eastb . . . 3E **19**
Mount Rd. BN20: Eastb . . . 1H **23**
Mt. View Ter. BN27: Hails . . . 3E **7**
Mowbray Ct. *BN21: Eastb . . . 5F 3*
(off Lascelles Ter.)
Moy Av. BN22: Eastb . . . 2A **20**
Mulberry Cl. BN22: Eastb . . . 2G **15**
Mulberry Ct. *BN26: Pole . . . 5C 8*
(off Walnut Wlk.)
MULBROOKS . . . 6E **7**
Musgrave Collection . . . 2D **20**
Myrtle Rd. BN22: Eastb . . . 1D **20**

N

Naomi Cl. BN20: Eastb . . . 6G **19** (5B **2**)
Nelson Dr. BN23: Eastb . . . 1E **21**
Netherfield Av. BN23: Lang . . . 3F **17**
Nevill Av. BN22: Eastb . . . 4G **15**
Neville Rd. BN22: Eastb . . . 3B **20**
New Barn Cl. BN27: Hails . . . 3E **7**
New College Cl. BN23: Lang . . . 1C **16**
New Derby Ho. BN23: Eastb . . . 6D **16**
Newick Rd. BN20: Eastb . . . 1E **19**
New Langney Ct. BN23: Lang . . . 4E **17**
New Pl. BN21: Eastb . . . 4F **19**
New Rd. BN22: Eastb . . . 3B **20** (1G **3**)
(not continuous)
BN26: Pole . . . 5D **8**
BN27: Hell . . . 3D **4**
Newton Pk. BN27: Hails . . . 2F **7**
New Upperton Rd.
BN21: Eastb . . . 3G **19**
New Vs. *BN26: Pole . . . 5D 8*
(off Western Av.)
Nicholson Ct. BN23: Lang . . . 4E **17**
Nightingale Cl. BN23: Lang . . . 3C **16**
Nodes La. BN27: Mag D . . . 3H **5**
Norfolk Ct. *BN22: Eastb . . . 3C 20*
(off Redoubt Rd.)
Norman Rd. BN24: Pev B . . . 5B **12**
NORMAN'S BAY . . . 1H **13**
**Norman's Bay Camping &
Caravanning Pk.**
BN24: Nor B . . . 2F **13**
Normans Bay Cvn. Pk.
BN24: Nor B . . . 1G **13**
Norman's Bay Station (Rail) . . . 1G **13**
North Av. BN20: Eastb . . . 2D **18**
Northbourne Rd. BN22: Eastb . . . 6B **16**
North Cl. BN26: Pole . . . 4D **8**
Nth. Crescent Ind. Est.
BN27: Hails . . . 2C **6**
Northern Av. BN26: Pole . . . 4D **8**
Northfield BN26: Pole . . . 6B **8**
Nth. Heath Cl. BN27: Hails . . . 5E **5**
Northiam Rd. BN20: Eastb . . . 3E **19**
BN21: Eastb . . . 3E **19**
North Rd. BN24: Pev B . . . 5B **12**
North St. BN21: Eastb . . . 5B **20** (2G **3**)
BN27: Hails, Hell . . . 2B **4**
(Church Rd.)
BN27: Hails . . . 1D **6**
(High St.)

Russet Cl. BN26: Pole 5E **9**
Rustington Ct.
BN20: Eastb 1H **23** (6D **2**)
Rutland Cl. BN21: Eastb 1F **19**
Rutland Ct. BN23: Lang 4E **17**
Ruxley Ct. BN23: Lang 3D **16**
Rydal Way BN23: Lang 1B **16**
Rye Cl. BN26: Pole 4E **9**
Ryefield Cl. BN21: Will 6E **15**
Rye St. BN22: Eastb 1D **20**
Rylstone Rd. BN22: Eastb 3C **20**

S

Sackville Rd. BN22: Eastb 3H **15**
BN27: Hails 3E **7**
Saffrons Ct.
BN20: Eastb 5G **19** (4B **2**)
Saffrons Ga.
BN20: Eastb 5H **19** (4C **2**)
Saffrons Mead
BN20: Eastb 5H **19** (4C **2**)
Saffrons Pk.
BN20: Eastb 6G **19** (5A **2**)
Saffrons Rd.
BN21: Eastb 4G **19** (2B **2**)
St Aidans Ct. BN22: Eastb 2C **20**
St Andrews Cl. BN27: Hails 6C **4**
St Annes Rd. BN20: Will 2D **14**
BN21: Eastb 3G **19**
St Anthony's Av. BN23: Eastb 5E **17**
ST ANTHONY'S HILL **6D 16**
St Aubyn's Rd.
BN22: Eastb 4B **20** (1H **3**)
St Boswells Cl. BN27: Hails 1C **6**
St Brelades *BN21: Eastb 4G 3*
(off Trinity Pl.)
St Clements Ct. BN21: Eastb 1F **19**
St Davids Cl. BN22: Eastb 1F **15**
St Denys BN21: Eastb 3G **19**
St Georges BN21: Eastb 3E **19**
St George's Rd. BN22: Eastb 3B **20**
St Gregory Cl.
BN20: Eastb 1G **23** (6A **2**)
St Helena Ct. BN21: Eastb 3G **19**
St Ives Ct. BN21: Eastb 3H **19**
St James BN24: Nor B 1H **13**
St James Rd. BN22: Eastb 3C **20**
St John's Dr. BN24: W'ham 5E **11**
St Johns Ho. BN20: Eastb 6C **2**
St John's Rd. BN20: Eastb 1G **23**
BN26: Pole 5C **8**
St Kilda Mans. *BN21: Eastb 1C 2*
(off Upperton Rd.)
St Kitts Dr. BN23: Eastb 6G **17**
St Lawrence M. BN23: Eastb 4G **17**
St Lawrence Pl. BN23: Eastb 4G **17**
St Lawrence Way
BN23: Eastb 4G **17**
St Leonard's Pl. BN20: Eastb 4E **19**
St Leonard's Rd.
BN21: Eastb 4H **19** (1D **2**)
St Leonards Ter. BN26: Pole 4B **8**
St Lucia Wlk. BN23: Eastb 5F **17**
St Martins Rd. BN22: Eastb 2F **15**
St Mary's BN26: Pole 5E **9**
St Mary's Av. BN27: Hails 2E **7**
St Mary's Cl. BN22: Will 3D **14**
St Mary's Cotts.
BN20: Eastb 4F **19** (1A **2**)
St Marys Ct.
BN21: Eastb 4F **19** (1A **2**)
St Mary's Rd. BN21: Eastb 3F **19**
St Marys Wlk. *BN27: Hails 2E 7*
(off High St.)
St Mellion Cl. BN27: Hails 1B **6**
St Michaels Cl. BN24: Sto C 5A **10**
St Nicholas Cl. BN24: Pev 5H **11**
St Paul's Cl. BN22: Eastb 2F **15**
St Philips Av. BN22: Eastb 2B **20**
St Ritas BN20: Eastb 6F **19** (6A **2**)
St Vincents Pl.
BN20: Eastb 6G **19** (6A **2**)
St Wilfred's Grn. BN27: Hails 1E **7**
ST WILFRID'S HOSPICE 3H **19**
Salehurst Rd. BN21: Eastb 4E **19**
Salisbury Cl. BN22: Will 3E **15**
Salisbury Rd. BN20: Eastb 1E **23**
Saltmarsh La.
BN27: Down, Hails 5E **7**
Salvador Cl. BN23: Eastb 6F **17**
Samoa Way BN23: Eastb 3H **17**
Sancroft Rd. BN20: Eastb 4D **18**
Sanctuary, The BN20: Eastb 3D **18**
Sandbanks Cl. BN27: Hails 4C **6**
Sandbanks Gdns. BN27: Hails 4D **6**
Sandbanks Gro. BN27: Hails 3D **6**
Sandbanks Way BN27: Hails 3C **6**
Sandford M. *BN23: Lang 2D 16*
(off Pensford Dr.)
San Diego Way BN23: Eastb 4H **17**
Sandown Cl. BN23: Lang 1A **16**
Sandpiper Wlk. BN23: Lang 3C **16**
Sandwich St. BN22: Eastb 1C **20**
San Juan Ct. BN23: Eastb 6G **17**
Sanshaw Ct.
BN21: Eastb 4G **19** (1A **2**)
Santa Cruz Dr. BN23: Eastb 6F **17**
Santos Wharf BN23: Eastb 5F **17**
Saxby Cl. BN23: Lang 4E **17**
Saxon Ground BN21: Eastb 3G **19**
Saxon Pl. BN21: Eastb 1E **19**
SAYERLAND **3C 8**
Sayerland La. BN26: Pole 3C **8**
Sayerland Rd. BN26: Pole 4B **8**
Scanlan Cl. BN20: Will 2C **14**
Schofield Way BN23: Eastb 6F **17**
School La. BN26: Pole 4C **8**
Seabeach La. BN22: Eastb 2C **20**
Seaford Rd. BN20: Fris 2A **22**
BN22: Eastb 2C **20**
Seaforth Ct. BN20: Eastb 4E **19**
Sea Rd. BN24: Pev B 4B **12**
Seaside BN22: Eastb 4B **20** (1H **3**)
BN23: Eastb 6D **16**
Seaside Rd.
BN21: Eastb 5B **20** (3G **3**)
Seaside Rdbt. BN22: Eastb 6D **16**
Seaville Dr. BN23: Eastb 5D **16**
BN24: Pev B 4B **12**
Selby Rd. BN21: Eastb 2F **19**
Selmeston Ho. BN21: Eastb 3F **19**
Selmeston Rd. BN21: Eastb 6E **15**
Selsfield Cl. BN21: Eastb 1F **19**
Selwyn Dr. BN21: Eastb 3G **19**
Selwyn Ho. BN21: Eastb 3G **19**
Selwyn Pk. Ct. BN21: Eastb 3G **19**
Selwyn Rd. BN21: Eastb 3G **19**
Sevenoaks Rd. BN23: Lang 3B **16**
Seven Sisters Rd. BN22: Will . . .2D **14**
Seven Sisters Sheep Cen. **4B 22**
Shakespeare Wlk.
BN23: Lang 3E **17**
Shalfleet Cl. BN23: Lang 2B **16**
Shanklin Cl. BN23: Lang 1B **16**
Shannon Way BN23: Eastb 5F **17**
Sheen Rd. BN22: Eastb 3B **20**
Sheffield Pk. Way
BN23: Lang 1A **16**
Shelley Wlk. BN23: Lang 3E **17**
Shepham La. BN26: Pole 4E **9**
Shepherds Cl. BN22: Eastb 2H **15**
Sheppey Wlk. BN27: Hails 4C **4**
Sheraton Cl.
BN21: Eastb 5H **19** (4D **2**)
Sherbourne Ct. *BN21: Eastb 3F 19*
(off Upperton Rd.)
Sherwood Ct. *BN21: Eastb 3F 3*
(off Devonshire Pl.)
Sherwood Grn. BN27: Hails 3D **6**
Shinewater Ct. BN23: Lang 2B **16**
Shinewater La. BN23: Lang 2B **16**
(not continuous)
Shinewater Rdbt.
BN23: Eastb 4B **16**
Shipley Mill Cl. BN24: Sto C 6B **10**
Short Brow Cl. BN22: Will 2D **14**
Shortdean Pl. BN21: Eastb 3F **19**
Shortlands Cl. BN22: Will 4E **15**
Shropshire Ct. BN20: Eastb 6D **14**
Sidcup Cl. BN23: Lang 3D **16**
Sidley Rd. BN22: Eastb 3C **20**
Silverdale Ct.
BN20: Eastb 6H **19** (6D **2**)
BN27: Hails 1D **6**
Silverdale Rd.
BN20: Eastb 6G **19** (6B **2**)
Silver Strand E. BN23: Eastb 4G **17**
Silver Strand W. BN23: Eastb . . .4G **17**
Singleton Mill Rd.
BN24: Sto C 6C **10**
Slindon Cres. BN23: Lang 4E **17**
(not continuous)
Snapson's Drove
BN27: Hails, Rick 3H **7**
Snowdon Cl. BN23: Lang 2D **16**
Solly Ct. BN21: Eastb 4B **20** (1G **3**)
Solomons Cl. BN23: Eastb 3H **17**
Solway BN27: Hails 5C **4**
Somerset Ct. BN23: Lang 4E **17**
Somerville Cl. BN23: Eastb 6E **17**
Sorrel Cl. BN23: Lang 2C **16**
Sorrel Dr. BN23: Lang 1B **16**
Southampton Cl. BN23: Eastb . . .5F **17**
South Av. BN20: Eastb 2D **18**
Southbourne Rd.
BN22: Eastb 1C **20**
South Cliff BN20: Eastb 1H **23**
Sth. Cliff Twr. BN20: Eastb 1H **23**
South Cl. BN24: Pev B 3D **12**
BN27: Hails 3D **6**
South Coast Falconry & Conservation Cen. **2A 6**
Southdoen Ct. *BN27: Hails 2E 7*
(off Bellbanks Rd.)
Southdown Av. BN20: Will 2C **14**
Southdown Cotts. BN20: Will 2C **14**
Southdown Ho.
BN20: Eastb 6H **19** (6D **2**)
Southdown Rd. BN20: Eastb 6D **14**
South Elms
BN20: Eastb 6G **19** (6B **2**)
Southerden Cl. BN27: Hails 2E **7**
Southern Av. BN26: Pole 5D **8**
Southern Rd. BN22: Eastb 3H **15**
Southfield BN26: Pole 6B **8**
Southfields Ct. *BN21: Eastb 2C 2*
(off Southfields Rd.)
Southfields Rd.
BN21: Eastb 4G **19** (1B **2**)
Sth. Lynn Dr. BN21: Eastb 3H **19**
South Rd. BN27: Hails 3C **6**
South St. BN21: Eastb . . .5H **19** (3D **2**)
(not continuous)
South Vw. BN21: Eastb 3G **19**
Sovereign Cen. BN22: Eastb 1E **21**
Sovereign Ct. BN22: Eastb 2C **20**
SOVEREIGN HARBOUR **4G 17**
Sovereign Harbour Marina **5G 17**
Sovereign Harbour Retail Pk.
BN23: Eastb 4F **17**
Sovereign Ho. *BN21: Eastb 3G 3*
(off Grand Pde.)
Sovereign Rdbt. BN22: Eastb . . .1E **21**
Spencer Ct. *BN21: Eastb 4E 3*
(off Spencer Rd.)
Spencer Ho. *BN21: Eastb 4E 3*
(off Spencer Rd.)
Spencer Rd.
BN21: Eastb 5A **20** (4E **3**)
Spring Cl. BN20: Will 4D **14**
Springfield Cl. BN24: W'ham 5F **11**
Springfield Rd. BN22: Eastb 3B **20**
Spring Lodge Cl. BN23: Lang . . .3E **17**
Spruce Cl. BN22: Eastb 3F **15**
Spur Rd. BN26: Pole 6D **8**
Spurway Pk. BN26: Pole 6D **8**
Squab La. BN27: Mag D 2H **5**
Square, The BN24: Pev B 3D **12**
BN27: Hails 2C **6**
Stables La. *BN21: Eastb 2E 3*
(off Station St.)
Stafford Ct. *BN23: Lang 4E 17*
(off Etchingham Rd.)
Stafford Ho. *BN21: Eastb 2D 2*
(off Southfields Rd.)
Stanhope Ct. *BN20: Eastb 6C 2*
(off Silverdale Rd.)
Stanley Rd. BN22: Eastb 3B **20**
Stanmer Dr. BN22: Will 4F **15**
Stanmer Ho.
BN21: Eastb 5H **19** (4D **2**)
Stansted Rd. BN22: Eastb 3A **20**
Stanton Prior BN20: Eastb 1F **23**
Star Rd. BN21: Eastb 4G **19** (1A **2**)
Station App. BN22: Eastb 4H **15**
Station Pde. *BN21: Eastb 2D 2*
(off Upperton Rd.)
Station Rd. BN26: Pole 4C **8**
BN27: Hails 2D **6**
BN27: Hell 2C **4**
Station Rd. Ind. Est.
BN27: Hails 3E **7**
Station Rdbt.
BN21: Eastb 4H **19** (2D **2**)
Station St.
BN21: Eastb 4A **20** (2D **2**)
Staveley Ct. *BN20: Eastb 1G 23*
(off Staveley Rd.)
Staveley Mead *BN20: Eastb 1G 23*
(off Buxton Rd.)
Staveley Rd. BN20: Eastb 1G **23**
Steeple Grange BN21: Eastb 3G **19**
Stevenson Cl. BN23: Lang 2E **17**
Sth Cliff Av.
BN20: Eastb 6H **19** (6D **2**)
Stiles, The BN27: Hails 2E **7**
Stirling Ct. BN23: Lang 4E **17**
STONE CROSS **6A 10**
Stone Cross Towermill **6B 10**
Stonegate Cl. BN23: Lang 1A **16**
Stoney Down *BN20: Eastb 1G 23*
(off Milnthorpe Rd.)
Stoney La. BN27: Hails 2E **7**
Stour Cl. BN24: Sto C 6H **9**
Stringwalk, The BN27: Hails 2E **7**
Stroma Gdns. BN27: Hails 5B **4**
Stuart Av. BN21: Eastb 1E **19**
Stud Farm Stables, The
BN26: Pole 5A **8**
Sturdee Cl. BN23: Eastb 6F **17**
Sturton Pl. BN27: Hails 2D **6**
Suffolk Ct. BN22: Eastb 3C **20**
Sumach Cl. BN22: Eastb 3G **15**
Summer Ct. BN20: Eastb 2F **23**
BN27: Hails 1D **6**
Summerdown Cl.
BN20: Eastb 4F **19**
Summerdown La.
BN20: E Dean 2C **22**
Summerdown Rd.
BN20: Eastb 4E **19**
Summerfields Av. BN27: Hails . . .1D **6**
Summerheath Rd.
BN27: Hails 1D **6**
SUMMER HILL **6C 6**
Summer Hill La. BN27: Hails 6B **6**
Summerlands Rd. BN22: Will . . .3D **14**
Sunningdale Cl. BN27: Hails 6C **4**
Sun Patch BN27: Hails 2E **7**
Sunset Cl. BN24: Pev B 3C **12**
Sunstar La. BN26: Pole 5A **8**
Susan's Rd.
BN21: Eastb 4A **20** (1F **3**)
Sussex Av. BN27: Hails 1D **6**
Sussex Cl. BN27: Hails 1D **6**
Sussex Ct. BN22: Eastb 2B **20**
Sussex Gdns. BN20: E Dean 2C **22**
Sussex Ho. *BN21: Eastb 3F 3*
(off Hartington Pl.)
Sussex Mans. *BN21: Eastb 3E 3*
(off Cornfield Ter.)
Sutton Ho. *BN20: Eastb 6B 2*
(off Meads Rd.)
Sutton Rd.
BN21: Eastb 4A **20** (2E **3**)
Swale Cl. BN24: Sto C 6A **10**
Swallow Cl. BN23: Lang 3B **16**
Swan Barn Bus. Cen.
BN27: Hails 3F **7**
Swan Barn Cvn. Site
BN27: Down 4F **7**
Swanley Cl. BN23: Lang 3D **16**
Swan Rd. BN27: Hails 3E **7**
Swinburne Av. BN22: Will 2D **14**
SWINGATE CROSS **2D 4**
Sycamore Cl. BN22: Eastb 2F **15**
Sycamore Dr. BN27: Hails 4D **6**
Sycamores, The BN21: Eastb . . .3H **19**
Sydney Rd.
BN22: Eastb 4B **20** (1G **3**)

T

Taddington Ho. *BN22: Eastb 3C 20*
(off Taddington Rd.)
Taddington Rd. BN22: Eastb 3C **20**
Tamarack Cl. BN22: Eastb 3F **15**
Tamar Cl. BN24: Sto C 6A **10**
Tanbridge Rd. BN23: Lang 3F **17**
Tanneries, The BN27: Mag D 3H **5**
Tas Combe Way BN20: Will 3D **14**
Tasmania Way BN23: Eastb 3G **17**
Tavistock *BN21: Eastb 4F 3*
(off Devonshire Pl.)
Teal Ct. BN27: Hails 2G **7**
Telscombe Rd. BN23: Lang 3F **17**
Tennis Cl. BN27: Hails 2D **6**
Tennyson Wlk. BN23: Lang 2E **17**
Tenterden Cl. BN23: Lang 3D **16**
Terminus Bldgs. *BN21: Eastb 2D 2*
(off Upperton Rd.)
Terminus Pl. *BN27: Hails 2E 7*
(off Station Rd.)
Terminus Rd.
BN21: Eastb 4H **19** (2E **3**)
(not continuous)
Thackeray Cl. BN23: Lang 2E **17**
Thorn Lodge *BN21: Eastb 4E 3*
(off Spencer Rd.)
Thornton Ct.
BN21: Eastb 4B **20** (1G **3**)
Thornwood
BN21: Eastb 4H **19** (1D **2**)
Thornwood Cl. BN22: Eastb 3G **15**
Thorpe, The
BN20: Eastb 6H **19** (6C **2**)
Thurrock Cl. BN20: Will 2C **14**
Tidebrook Gdns. BN23: Lang 3F **17**
(not continuous)